Preparing
The **Way**

31 DAYS FOR
ADVENT
FOR GROUP OR PERSONAL USE

Preparing
The *Way*

CWR

Derek Tidball

Contents

Introduction

I am not sure whether the neighbours were amazed or just amused. My father, a retired painter and decorator, had come to stay and was repainting our garage door while he was with us. It needed it! The curious thing, however, was that he spent days rubbing it down, repairing it and undercoating it. We thought he was never going to complete the job. But once he had done the preparation, it took him no time to put the top coat on. It was a quality job and would last for years before it needed further attention. 'The secret of any successful job,' he would explain when asked, 'lies in the preparation. Most people skimp on the preparation, go straight to the final stages, and end up with something that needs repainting all too soon. They get the job they deserve because they haven't prepared it properly.'

When you think of it, much of life is spent in preparation! We're preparing for exams, preparing for marriage, preparing to buy a house, preparing to go on holiday, preparing for a concert, preparing to cook dinner, preparing for guests to arrive. The preparation often takes longer than the activity itself. We have a whole battery of words to describe the process: we study for an exam, rehearse for a concert, train for a race, plan for a holiday, get ready for guests, and so on.

The greatest thing most couples prepare for, of course, is the arrival of a baby. In anticipation we redecorate rooms, buy cots and car seats, become frequent visitors to shops selling baby clothes and equipment, get out the knitting needles, read books, consult lists of names, go to prenatal classes, dream ... and so it goes on. The lack of preparation is usually considered a great hindrance. And all the time the baby is undergoing his or her own preparation in the womb.

The most famous birth in history was preceded by the longest and most minute preparation of all. From conception to birth is usually nine months – nine months in which the parents are alerted to the need to get ready. But preparation for the birth of the baby in Bethlehem began before the worlds were made. Those who were sensitive to the ways of God keenly anticipated the birth centuries before it occurred. We're familiar with the preparation of Mary, Joseph and others nearer the time. But we're less familiar with how God prepared the politicians and powerful people to orchestrate events so that Jesus would be born, not in Nazareth, but in Bethlehem. No birth has ever been prepared for as much as the birth of Jesus.

Some years later His relative John cried in the desert, 'Prepare a straight pathway for the Lord's coming!' (John 1:23, NLT), or in old-style language, 'Prepare ye the way of the Lord!' Now, as then, we are called to prepare the way for the Lord's coming, first by preparing ourselves spiritually to enter fully into the story and significance of His first coming, and then by preparing for His coming again. Here is a story in which we're all called to be participants, not spectators.

This Advent book looks at how God prepared the way for the birth of Jesus and how the cast of the original Christmas story played their part. But it also invites us to prepare for Jesus' coming again into our lives.

There's so much preparation to be done for Christmas. There are cards to write (or emails to send), presents to buy, large quantities of food to purchase, trees and rooms to decorate, beds to prepare … In it all, let's give attention to preparing ourselves spiritually, not as an afterthought, but as a priority. Let's hear and respond to the call to 'Make way for Christ the King'.[1]

How to use this book

This Advent book may be used in two ways: personally and in groups. For every day of December there is something to consider or discuss that can be used for either personal or group reflection and prayer. Then, at the end of every week, there are a few questions which look back on the studies and serve as the basis for a discussion in a home group or other small group setting. They're not an examination paper! You don't have to answer them all! They are a means of opening up a discussion about the extraordinary way in which God prepared for the salvation of the world through the baby of Bethlehem.

The studies are grouped into five sections. They start by looking at the earliest hints of the preparation for Jesus' coming. Next we look at the preparation through a wide-angle lens, and see how

God arranged the events of history in such a way that His coming occurred at a key moment. Following that we look at the main cast of people – those who were most closely involved in the story – before picking up on the wider cast in the story, many of whom arrived once the birth had taken place. Finally we're reminded, as we should be by Advent, that Christ is also going to come again, and that we need to be prepared for His second arrival, this time in splendour.

Note

1. The phrase is based on Graham Kendrick's song, 'Make way, make way, for Christ the King'.

The Saviour Promised Long

Preparing the way of the Lord ... a long time ago

Prospective parents normally have nine months' notice of the arrival of a baby. The months are usually filled with frenetic activity as the preparations are made. In Jesus' case, although Mary and Joseph may have had the usual period of notice, the preparations began long before the pregnancy. The Old Testament Scriptures had for centuries prophesied of the coming of the Messiah, and the preparations began way back in eternity.

These days we can watch any number of films in the comfort of our homes on our televisions, but this can sometimes be a poor substitute for watching a film on a big cinema screen, especially if panoramic scenery or supreme artistry is involved. Seeing it on a wide screen enhances our wonder. The Bible portrays the birth of Jesus both close up and on a wide screen. We begin with the wide-screen picture – a picture that should increase our wonder at God's extraordinary grace.

1 Dec

Let us begin ...

Bible reading John 1:1–18

When it comes to children, you can find out when they were conceived and will never be allowed to forget the day they were born, even if you want to! Their story begins at the beginning. But when it comes to Jesus, when exactly was the beginning?

Matthew begins with Joseph discovering the news that his fiancée, as we would call her, was pregnant, although he also traces Jesus' ancestry back to Abraham. Luke begins with family news – the news of Christ's relative John's birth – but essentially focuses on the child's arrival in Bethlehem. Mark, as always, was in a hurry. He doesn't even mention the birth of Jesus but pitches straight in to the time when Jesus was baptised and began His public ministry. But for John, these writers haven't begun at the beginning. They come into the story too late. If you really want to understand the baby born in Bethlehem you've got to start way back before the world was created: 'in the beginning'.

Echoing the opening verses of Genesis, John tells us the One who 'became flesh and made his dwelling among us' (v.14) did not start His life on the day He was born, or even at conception, but that, like God Himself, there never was a time when He was not. The baby of Bethlehem is eternal.

Babies derive their life from their parents. But not Jesus. Everything ever created, including every human being, derives its life from Him: 'without him nothing was made that has been made. In him was life' (vv.3–4). He was not the recipient of life but the source and giver of life.

John highlights several things about this amazing claim. Jesus creates life because He was not only 'with God' at the start (so to speak) but indeed 'was God' (v.1). His deity gives Him the power and the desire to create life. The life He creates is good and wholesome, characterised by light, not darkness (v.4). Yet people resisted the light, causing a problem that needed a remedy (vv.5,10–12). The remedy came through God's Word. We express ourselves by using words, but 'the Word' that God spoke wasn't the sort of word we usually think of; it was a human being: Jesus.

'The Word' stayed around for a good time – that's what 'made his dwelling among us' means (v.14) – and when people encountered this Word, they came to believe He could repair what had gone wrong by enabling them to be recreated, born anew, in God's family. As they examined 'the Word' they saw His life as 'full of grace and truth' (v.14). It wasn't just that they couldn't fault Him. It was rather that love, mercy, wisdom, truth and integrity poured out of Him.

The preparation started before time, as we know it, began; before creation, as we experience it, existed; and before humans, like us, walked the earth. God's plan, from eternity, was that this immense, mind-boggling, awesome, powerful and eternal Word should become a helpless baby in Bethlehem. Wow!

To consider or discuss

• Read today's passage again, slowly and prayerfully. What phrases in it catch your attention, what questions arise in your mind? How does the passage increase your wonder at the baby of Bethlehem? Have you turned that wonder into praise?

2 Dec

Beginning in time

Bible reading Genesis 3:14–15

Although the story of Jesus begins in eternity we may still ask, 'So when did it begin in time?' Even that's difficult to answer because it all depends what you mean by time. To start with His conception or His birth is to start far too late, even though we are speaking of a real baby who has a birthday that can be dated in history. His story began centuries before that with God preparing the way from the beginning.

Judges on the TV programme *Strictly Come Dancing* have been known to comment to contestants, 'You got off on the wrong foot.' So, it seems, did Adam and Eve, the father and mother of us all. God created them as responsible human beings, able to make moral choices, as distinct from robots who had no free will. Yet, in spite of all the initial advantages of their close relationship with God, when presented with a choice by the serpent, they made the wrong choice. They disregarded God's instruction and ate the fruit of the one tree He had forbidden them to touch. So the relationship with God broke down, with further dire consequences for their relationship with each other, for the earth they inhabited, and their future life (vv.14–24).

What was to be done? Was that it? Should God write off humanity as a failed experiment? Was creation a good idea that had gone wrong and was irreparable? Or could the damage be repaired, the relationship restored, the disobedience redeemed and the situation rescued? Without delay God puts a rescue plan into operation. Even while announcing His justly deserved sentence, He shows Adam and Eve a sign of His grace by clothing them (v.21). And He introduces a note of hope. The catastrophe was not irrecoverable.

The gospel note comes when God speaks to the serpent. In condemning him to crawl in the dust, God adds, 'And I will put enmity between you and the woman, and between your offspring and hers; he will crush your head, and you will strike his heel' (v.15). Originally these words may have meant no more to them than that although there would be perpetual hostility between humanity and the serpent (the representative of evil), there was the hope that eventually humanity would triumph over evil and finally crush it.

When Christ came, however, people looked at those words with fresh eyes, as if the cataracts had been removed and they could see the meaning clearly. The serpent was the personification (or whatever the animal equivalent is) of evil. He represented Satan (Rom. 16:20), who constantly fought against human beings, waging a war on them that would lead to their destruction, as history documents all too clearly. But the warfare reached its culmination when a woman's offspring engaged in a battle that would result in the complete defeat of Satan. The woman was Mary, and the offspring, Jesus. Satan would stalk and harry Jesus throughout His public life, until His attacks reached their climax when Jesus was crucified. On the cross 'the offspring' suffered real hurt – but it was as if only His heel had been injured. The damage inflicted on Satan was far greater. An injured heel is nothing in comparison with a crushed head. The one is not fatal, the other is.

The preparations for the rescue mission involving the birth of Jesus began in the Garden of Eden.

To consider or discuss

• This is the earliest announcement of the gospel. As soon as the problem arose, God planned the solution. But let's not underestimate 'the serpent'. What evidence do you see of his evil work in your own circle, and how might the power of Christ overcome him? Thank God for the long-term preparation from which we benefit today.

3 Dec

Signpost to the future

Bible reading Isaiah 7:1–17

It's amazing how poor we are at predicting the future. Stories abound of people who got it wrong. Margaret Thatcher famously said there would be no woman prime minister in her lifetime. Alvin Toffler's *Future Shock*, a cult book on the future published as recently as 1970, hardly mentioned the computer, which has had a greater impact on our lives than anything else since then. At the end of the twentieth century the respected social commentator Francis Fukuyama predicted that liberal democracy had triumphed and brought peace, only for us to walk slap bang into the rise of terrorism and a new conflict with militant Islam. Signposts to the future often fail to point in the right direction! But not the signpost Isaiah gave.

Isaiah was speaking around 734 years before the birth of Christ, when the kings of Syria and Israel were trying to persuade King Ahaz of Judah to join them in what would have been a ruinous campaign against Assyria, the newish powerful kid on the block at the time. Ahaz rightly refused, but it was a tense time even so, and one in which he needed encouragement to 'keep calm' (v.4) and 'stand firm' (v.9). How could Ahaz be sure the guidance he received from Isaiah was the advice he should trust when other prophets were offering different advice? God gives Ahaz a sign, whether he wanted it or not (and it looks as if he didn't!): 'The virgin will be with child and will give birth to a son, and will call him Immanuel' (v.14). The point was that before this child grew up and could distinguish between good and bad food, in other words in a matter of just a few years, Syria and Israel would see their lands devastated.

While the child's mother reacts by rejoicing in the birth as a sign that God was with them and expresses faith, Ahaz refuses to trust and instead keeps on trying to work things out and appease Assyria with human strategies, with predictable consequences. He preferred not to have faith in God and rely on the words of His prophet. History would confirm the truth of Isaiah's words. Genuine prophets can provide true signposts to the future; what they predict comes about.

Isaiah doesn't name the son, but the belief grew that his words were about the birth of a royal son. In one respect this was a prophecy to be fulfilled soon, and possibly refers to King Hezekiah. But that's not the full story. Matthew 1:23 tells us that when Christians read these words they see a deeper meaning in them than Isaiah would ever have realised. Centuries later his words were to be fulfilled once again. In a world that continued to be in crisis, another unmarried young woman bore another child whom they could not but conclude was a sign that God was with them. Jesus was never called Immanuel (meaning 'God with us') to His face in His lifetime, but He constantly demonstrated that God was present among them through His teaching and His actions. God had come to live among them, to accomplish salvation for them, to overthrow the wicked and to trigger the start of a new age.

Isaiah's sign pointed to something that happened in his own lifetime, but equally it pointed beyond that to something of greater significance that was going to happen way in the future. This sign was not just for Judah but for all of us. Unlike many who predict the future, Isaiah didn't get it wrong. God was already at work, preparing the way for a virgin to conceive and bear a child.

To consider or discuss

- In a world of continuing crisis are you 'keeping calm' and 'standing firm' in faith because God continues with us (Matt. 28:20)? In that light, pray about the troubled events in our world today.

4 Dec

The government to come

Bible reading Isaiah 9:1–7

It's a majestic sight, mysterious and awesome. You've probably seen it. You may have been flying across the earth or just got up very early in the morning to witness it: the dawn, that is, and the rising of the sun. At first just a small streak of light pierces the darkness, but it grows and keeps on growing until darkness is banished and everything is light.

Isaiah's compatriots, especially those who lived in the north and were the first in line when Assyria invaded, felt they lived in deep darkness. But Isaiah promises the day will arrive when a royal son will come and change all that. He's so certain it will happen that rather than use the future tense he uses the past, as if it had happened already. 'The people walking in darkness *have seen* a great light; on those living in the land of deep darkness a light *has dawned*' (v.2, TNIV).

In his excitement, Isaiah fires off a volley of pictures of the transformation to come. A world of darkness will experience light (v.2).

A world of sorrow will rediscover joy (v.3). A world of slavery will encounter freedom (v.4). A world of strife will find peace (v.5). And how will this come about? How do we know it's more than wishful thinking on Isaiah's part?

The answer hinges on the birth of a son, yet to come (v.6). It's easy to dismiss a child as insignificant. But this child is destined to reign, and when He comes to power the world will be transformed. In contrast to conventional rulers, He will establish and uphold justice and righteousness. This child is none other than the successor to David, Israel's greatest and best king.

Royal babies get given several names to connect them with all the right people in their lineage. This royal baby has four names (v.6) which sum up who He is, what He's like, and what He does. All of them apply clearly to Jesus. He is a *Wonderful Counsellor*. His wisdom is evident. He demonstrates unfailing insight and understanding, makes prudent decisions and judicious rulings. He's a wonder of a Counsellor as well as being a Counsellor of wonderful things, as His daily encounters with men and women showed. He is *Mighty God*. His power and His divinity are evident. He does what God alone can do, like stilling storms, casting out demons, multiplying bread and fish, walking on water, healing the sick, forgiving sins and transforming the broken. He is the *Everlasting Father*. What a strange way of speaking about a yet-to-be-born baby. Yet both elements are seen fulfilled in Jesus. John tells us, as we've seen, that He was 'in the beginning' (John 1:1), and Jesus mysteriously claims, 'Before Abraham was born, I am!' (John 8:58). Not only is Jesus everlasting, but He also perpetually demonstrates the father heart of God. The claims about the kind of father God is – like those in Psalm 68:5 or 103:13 – come true in Him. Lastly, He is the *Prince of Peace*. His reign, unlike that of any other, will bring about peace not only between people, nations and races in conflict on earth but also between people and their God. It is a peacemaking, however, that is going to be accomplished at the cost of His own life (Col. 1:20).

God had the birth of Jesus well in hand way back in Isaiah's day. Now there's preparation!

To consider or discuss

- Pray through the titles of Jesus here, recalling incidents in the Gospels that fit them, and ask what they mean to you, today.

5 Dec

Roots and shoots

Bible reading Isaiah 11:1–9

Twice I have visited the hills in Australia after they've experienced the devastating bush fires that the extreme heat of an Australian summer can spark – once in Adelaide and more recently in Melbourne. Everything in the fire's path had been consumed: houses, machinery, people, plants, trees and animals alike. Tree trunks remained blackened, leaves burned, and the scene was one of utter desolation. Except, months later, tiny green shoots began poking through the charred remains of the forest, new leaves beginning to form. Nature was restoring life where once there was only destruction.

Isaiah pictured the future of Israel as a similar scene of devastation. The people's unfaithfulness meant that God would use Assyria to judge them (Isa. 7:18–8:8), and they would experience almost total destruction. It would be as if only a stump of a tree was left; nothing else. The fruit was cremated, the foliage withered, the branches hacked off, and the trunk cut down. But eventually the stump was going to put forth a shoot, a promising sign of a new beginning.

The trouble is Isaiah complicates this straightforward image and speaks not only of the shoot that will grow out of 'the stump of Jesse' but that this shoot is also a root. Confusing, or what? The explanation is, in fact, simple. Isaiah pictures a distant time when a new royal King would arise from the house of David – that's the shoot. But this King was not merely a son of David; He was at the

same time the origin or source of David's line – that's the root. He
may be from David's family but that family owes its very existence
to Him. He is the source of the royal line into which eventually He
would be born. The root is the shoot – the Messiah who was to
come and rescue Israel and the wider world from oppression and sin.
Roots take time to bed down in the earth and produce shoots above
the soil. So God planted this royal root a long time before the shoot
became evident.

Not content with the mere announcement, Isaiah tells us
something of the nature of this coming son of Jesse. The Spirit
would anoint Him 'big-time' (vv.2–3). In the Old Testament the Spirit
came upon people who were chosen to fulfil certain tasks, but none
ever had such a measure of the Spirit as the Messiah would. Look
at the seven-fold gift the Spirit would bestow on Him: wisdom,
understanding, counsel, power, knowledge, the fear of the Lord, and
delight in God.

Isaiah then talks about the way these characteristics of the Spirit
would work their way out in the Messiah's ministry. His judgments
would be anything but superficial. Reaching beneath the surface,
they would bring a true justice and righteousness into play that
would be of genuine benefit to the poor and the powerless. He
would put an end to the wickedness that enslaves and destroys, and
do so on a global scale. No mere shoot would have been adequate
to the task. 'The shoot' also needed to be 'the root' to achieve such a
mission.

Although the New Testament nowhere fully identifies Jesus with
these verses, there are regular echoes of them and the equation
is clear. The early Christians saw the unmistakable signs of a new
beginning in the Spirit-filled man from Nazareth, the son of David.

To consider or discuss

- Meditate on the seven-fold nature of the Spirit's resting on Jesus.
  How do you see these characteristics working out in His life and
  ministry?

6 Dec

O little town

Bible reading Micah 5:1–5

The day we planned to visit Bethlehem it was in lockdown. Workers were on strike and stone-throwing youths were rioting on the streets, so people had run indoors for safety. That's not unusual since the town has been one of the flashpoints between Palestinians and Israeli soldiers for years. Beside my desk I have an olive-wood carving of Jesus washing Peter's feet that was given to me by a key Christian leader who lives in Bethlehem. When he gave it to me he told me some harrowing stories of what the residents suffered and asked me not to forget their plight. The carol 'O little town of Bethlehem' may paint a picture of perfect calm and have us sing, 'how still we see Thee lie, above Thy deep and dreamless sleep', but the place now is anything but peaceful. And that connects us directly to the time when it first became clear that Bethlehem was being prepared as the Messiah's birthplace.

Most people know little about the prophet Micah (although they may be familiar with Micah 6:8), but every year they're likely to hear his words at a carol service: 'But you, Bethlehem Ephrathah, though you are small among the clans of Judah, out of you will come for me one who will be ruler over Israel, whose origins are from of old, from ancient times' (v.2). These words were first spoken in troubled times, when Israel was being attacked by Sennacherib. Realistically their future was bleak. Was there any hope they'd survive and, if so, where would they find it? Into this despair Micah injects a message of God's grace. There was hope, although deliverance wouldn't come immediately and it wouldn't come from the obvious place. The answer to their problems didn't lie in Jerusalem, the centre of power, but in Bethlehem.

Bethlehem was an insignificant little town some six miles to the southwest. Its name meant the 'house of bread'. It was situated in the district of Ephrathah, which meant 'fruitful'. Bethlehem had little to do with power politics but served merely as the bakery for Israel. The only significant thing about it was that it was David's home town. Like the town, David was at one time considered insignificant, the least in his family. But what God had done once, He was going to do again. If the great King David could come from this dead-end place then God could arrange for another ruler, who initially would be overlooked, to come from there.

The prophecy suggests several important things about this ruler besides His *humble origins*. It says He'd be a ruler 'for me', that is for God, suggesting that He wouldn't govern arrogantly or self-sufficiently but would rule under *God's direction*. His emergence would mean a *new beginning* for Israel. The past would be rolled away. Yet He isn't overthrowing everything from the past. In saying His 'origins are from of old, from ancient times' (v.2), Micah is telling us that He would be *revitalising David's rule*, as promised in 2 Samuel 7:13. When Jesus was born, Matthew announced this prophecy was coming true at last (Matt. 2:5).

So next time you sing the carol, don't get carried away with romantic dreams. Think of the real strife-torn situation of Bethlehem, and think of the miraculous way in which God devised an answer, right there, where the need was great and where it was least expected.

To consider or discuss

- Pray for peace in Bethlehem and, after reading Psalm 122, pray also for peace in Jerusalem.

7 Dec

The dawn breaks

Bible reading Malachi 4:1–6

British ambassadors have had the tradition of writing a final unvarnished dispatch to the Foreign Office as they come to the end of their service and enter retirement. These dispatches reveal what really mattered to the ambassadors and what they really thought about things, and often proved brutally honest. Matthew Parris recently published some of them in a surprisingly popular book called *Parting Shots*.[2] Today we look at the parting shot of the Old Testament – the last words spoken by an inspired prophet before John cried in the desert, 'Prepare the way of the Lord.'

Malachi lived 400 years or so before Christ came. He was a hard-hitting prophet with some stern things to say about the people's unfaithfulness to God, but, as with Amos and similar straight-talking prophets, his last words are words of grace, not condemnation. True, Malachi is still realistic about the terrifying consequences that will follow if people ignore his call to stop robbing God (vv.1,6). But look at the positive message he leaves.

Malachi promises that 'the day is coming' (v.1) when, first, *the people will be refined*. Malachi had spoken before about the refiner's fire (3:2–4). Reusing the picture, he promises a future when all the arrogant (see Luke 1:51–52) and evildoers will be removed from among the people, as if they were impurities skimmed off the heated metal in the refiner's fire. At last people would be cleansed and united in their purity.

Second, he looks forward to a time when *the sun will rise* (v.2), banishing the darkness of failure and despair and bringing health and wholeness in its wake. The idea of healing being in the sun's wings suggests the sun as a dynamic and lively power for good rather than something inert, motionless and dead. In the middle of winter we long for the sun to shine and overcome the dark nights and gloomy days. Israel had lived through a spiritual winter and would do so for some centuries yet. But when Christ came, the light would shine again and renewed health would follow.

Third, Malachi says that day would be instantly recognisable because *the prophet would be revived*. Elijah had an enormous and positive impact in confronting the nation and causing it to face up to its situation and repent. Some time in the future another Elijah would come, and this event would immediately precede the day of the Lord. When John the Baptist was conceived, the angel told his father that he would 'go on before the Lord, in the spirit and power of Elijah' (Luke 1:17). And when John began to preach, people saw him as fulfilling this prophecy, even if he resisted their claims (John 1:21–23). His ministry seems modelled on that of Elijah as he prepared the way for the ministry of Jesus, 'the sun of righteousness'.

The final words, then, before the voice of true prophecy fell silent for four centuries, were not about judgment falling but about hope promised. God longed to refine and redeem His people. So a last appeal is made for them to repent and the ultimate sign is offered: that the day would dawn when John the Baptist preached repentance and Jesus announced the arrival of God's kingdom (Mark 1:15).

To consider or discuss

- Think of Jesus as 'the sun of righteousness' who brings healing. Turn the image over prayerfully in your mind. What does it mean to you? What testimony do you have of God's healing?

For group discussion

This week's readings have taken us through some of the key prophecies that predicted the birth of the Messiah. No child's birth has ever been expected so keenly or foretold in such accurate detail as that of Jesus. Share your general reactions to the prophecies you've read. Why are such prophecies important and how do they strengthen our faith?

1 Do we make Jesus too personal? Personal Saviour though He is, this week's readings reveal a Christ whose preparation began way back in history and whose redemption was concerned with the affairs of nations, not just individuals. Discuss whether or not we're in danger of seeing everything about the faith through too narrow a personal lens instead of on the wide screen.

2 Which of the prophecies we've read this week about the coming of Jesus mean most to you, and why?

3 Together, list the key things about the coming of Christ you have learned in these readings. How do they help you in your Christian life? Can you turn them into a prayer?

4 What other prophecies about the coming of Christ in the Old Testament have we omitted? What do these prophecies tell us about Jesus?

To guide you in praying

The prophets looked forward to the coming of the Messiah with intense longing. The thirteenth-century carol 'O come, O come, Immanuel' expresses the joy that His coming would bring: 'captive Israel' would be ransomed, 'lonely exile' would be overcome, people would be set free from tyranny, the 'depths of hell' and 'the long night's lingering gloom' would be dispelled, and the 'shadows of the tomb' would be pierced.

Try to capture something of the intense desire of the prophets, and the carol, as you pray for those who need to be set free from captivity, exile, tyranny and fear, whether it be of a political, emotional or spiritual kind.

Note

2 Matthew Parris, *Parting Shots* (London: Viking, 2010).

Hope of the World

Preparing the way of the Lord
... in the real world

When we think of the preparations for the coming of
Christ, our minds usually go either to the Old Testament
prophets or to the people, like Mary and Joseph, who are
most closely involved. But there is a wider picture we need
to take in. It wasn't just the individual people who needed
preparing, but the world – the real broken world of politics,
economics and social oppression. Often we skip over
the details, but the Gospel writers spend time telling us
what was happening on the world stage and who was in
power when Jesus was born. This, too, was all part of the
meticulous preparation for the Messiah's birth. And that's
the theme for this week's readings.

8 Dec

It's time!

Bible reading Galatians 3:26–4:7

For some things, timing is all-important. The art of preparing a roast dinner is to make sure the meat is cooked and the potatoes, vegetables and Yorkshire puddings are all ready at the same time. It's no good having one dish ready before the rest. It will only spoil. It's even worse when it comes to preparing, say, for a wedding. The ceremony needs to be arranged, the registrar or clergyman available, the wedding dress made, the cake baked, the venue for the reception booked, the invitations sent out, the tables prepared ... all for the same day. How many bridal families wake up after months of preparation and heave a sigh of relief that the day has come at last! The time to which people have been looking forward for so long has arrived. And when it does come, things change. The marriage takes place and the couple cease to be single individuals and become husband and wife. The wedding breakfast is eaten and people are fed. The arrival of the time means something decisive happens.

Paul says something similar about the birth of Jesus: 'when the time had fully come, God sent his Son, born of a woman, born under law, to redeem those under law', so that we might receive adoption as children (4:4–5). Paul doesn't mean God had been idly ticking off the days in His diary until the day of Christ's birth materialised. There's much more to it than that. Paul means God had been making preparations until the critical moment arrived when all was ready for Christ to be born and everything would change. In cooking terms, God had brought everything to the boil! But Paul doesn't use a cooking illustration; he uses a family one. He develops the illustration he's just used of a son ceasing to be a minor and coming of age (4:1–2). Roman law fixed this at the age of 14. You could neither speed it up nor slow it down. It would happen in 'the fulness of ... time' (AV). And when it did, things changed not only for the son but for everyone else in the household as well.

Why did God call 'It's time!'? Some say this was because the world was in a state of readiness to receive Jesus Christ. They point to the *pax Romana* to suggest that the birth of Jesus took place at an opportune time when the gospel could easily spread around the civilised world since the peace and infrastructure created by the Roman empire facilitated communication. But that doesn't seem to be quite Paul's point. Looking at the flow of his argument, his point is somewhat different. He means rather that just as when an individual child reaches the age of majority and is considered an adult and is no longer subject to the guardian, he enters a new chapter in his life, so when Christ was born the world entered a new stage of history. The age of salvation dawned. The new era commenced in which people could relate through grace to God as sons and daughters and no longer needed to relate to Him as slaves under the law. It was time for the future age – the age of the Messiah, to which people had long looked forward – to begin.

True, not all the benefits of this new age have been completely realised as yet. So Paul is also able to write that the plan Jesus began to put into operation at His birth will be 'put [fully] into effect when the times will have reached their fulfilment', that is, in the still future day when Christ returns again (Eph. 1:10). But after His first coming the world would never be the same again. The time had come at last when a new and decisive stage of its relationship with God had been reached. The age of grace had dawned. Sonship, rather than slavery, was available to all. At that time, the plan of salvation made a decisive and irreversible breakthrough, even though it is yet to be fully accomplished.

Thank God for the day when He called 'It's time!' The world could not have struggled on in slavery much longer without the good news of freedom and salvation. Nor need it do so now. 'I tell you, now is the time of God's favour, now is the day of salvation' (2 Cor. 6:2).

To consider or discuss

- Read today's passage carefully and ask yourself whether you feel like a slave or a child of God. Ask God (or thank Him) for the assurance that you have been adopted.

9 Dec

What's in a list?

Bible Reading Matthew 1:1–17

Some people love writing lists, but even the enthusiasm of the most ardent writer of 'to do' lists tends to wane when they're confronted by a long list of names. When I worked in a theological college, the registrar would give us a list of the names of incoming students at the beginning of the academic year. At first they would mean little to us. But as we got to know the people whose names were on the list, those lists came alive. The Bible seems fond of giving us lists of names. Not only do they give us the names of real people; the lists are also full of significance. Matthew begins his Gospel with one such list.

For Matthew, it was important to establish the legitimacy of Jesus' claim to be the Messiah. The Messiah was the royal King and long-expected Deliverer of Israel who would 'save his people from their sins' (v.21). If Jesus was to be the legitimate Messiah, He needed to come from the right bloodline. Two connections were of particular importance. He had to be a 'son of Abraham', the father of the nation and first recipient of God's covenant with Israel. And He had to be an 'heir of David', the greatest king Israel has ever had, and the one to whom God had said, 'I will establish the throne of his kingdom for ever' (2 Sam. 7:13). So Matthew sets about investigating the family line of Jesus.

Matthew comes up with a schematic way of presenting his results. His approach is like a map of the London Underground. The map is helpful in giving us the right information and a true representation of how things connect up, even though the actual reality is a good deal more complex. The Underground map can't be taken as giving us, for example, the actual distances between stations, but it gives us an accurate idea of where they are in relation to each other and which line goes where. So it is with Matthew's account of Jesus' family tree. He places Jesus' forerunners in three groups, each consisting of 14 generations. The first is from Abraham to David (vv.2–6a); the second from David to the Exile (vv.6b–11); and the third from the Exile to Jesus (vv.12–16). He works forwards from Abraham through David to Jesus, and then looks backward from Jesus, through David, to Abraham (v.17). In doing this he sees Jesus as the culmination of history. With Him a new beginning occurs, and nothing would ever be the same again. Everything leads up to the coming of Christ and, subsequently, everything would take its cue from Him.

Here is God's way of fulfilling the promise to David. There were times when His plan looked very unlikely to come to fruition. The first phase ended with the climax of royal power under David, but the second phase was a painful reminder of the loss of royal power. The third phase is the restoration period, when Israel was restored to its homeland, a chastened and much reduced people. But to be honest, that didn't seem to live up to the promise. And yet God was in control all the time, His plan working itself out. His sovereignty was not to be doubted. His purposes were indeed coming to fulfilment: 'God is working His purpose out as year succeeds to year', as Arthur Ainger's hymn puts it. Whatever it looked like, the preparations were advancing and all would be ready for 'Jesus the Messiah' to be born.

To consider or discuss

- Look back on your life and recall a time when all seemed to be going wrong but then you subsequently found God was in control all along. Do you resent it or see the providence of God in it? Thank God, even for these bewildering experiences.

10 Dec

The list revisited

Bible reading Matthew 1:1–17

Working out your family tree has recently become very popular.
There are plenty of tools on the internet that can help you do it. It
may seem a straightforward thing to do. You just have to trace who
'begat' whom (to use the Authorised Version word), and there you
have it. But anyone who's tried to do it knows it's not as easy as
it seems. Some leads become dead ends. Records are incomplete.
Families constantly use the same Christian names so you can't sort
out who's who. And so on.

The other difficulty is that you're liable to uncover some secrets
best kept hidden. Skeletons have a habit of popping out of cupboards
and scandals are rediscovered and revived. The amazing thing about
the list of Jesus' ancestors is that there's clearly no attempt to cover
anything up. In fact, by the route it takes and the names it includes,
it almost seems to make a point of saying that Jesus had His fair
share of failures, embarrassments and scandals in His family tree.
Many of us would find that encouraging in itself.

In the second group of names (vv.6b–11), mention is made of
Rehoboam, who lost more than half of Solomon's kingdom, of Asa
and Hezekiah, who were great kings to start with but then messed
up, of Jehoram, who was wicked through and through, of Manasseh,
who was plain evil much of the time, and of Jeconiah, who saw
Israel go into exile. Yet Jesus, the Saviour, was born into this line of
ne'er-do-wells.

The most surprising thing, however, is the inclusion of four
women's names in the list. At the time, the family line would have
been traced through the male line, so what are they doing here?
When we see who the women are, the mystery deepens. There is
Tamar (v.3), who acted as a prostitute and enticed her father-in-law
into bed to expose his callous chauvinist indifference to her plight
(see Gen. 38). There is Rahab (v.5), a rank outsider from Jericho who
demonstrated faith in Israel's God and was rewarded for it, but may

have been a brothel-keeper by trade (see Josh. 2). Next comes Ruth from Moab (v.5), another outsider who suffered tragically through bereavement. But she loyally followed her grieving mother-in-law back to Bethlehem and took the initiative in manipulating men into fulfilling their family responsibilities towards them (see the book that bears her name). Finally there is Uriah's wife (v.6), who was almost certainly a Hittite, like her husband. The failure to use her personal name and the way she's introduced suggests the focus is not on her adultery (see 2 Sam. 11) but on her being a foreigner.

Each of these remarkable women faced tough and messy circumstances not of their own making which resulted in their entering into unconventional unions with men. Yet they were honoured as women who took the initiative and acted with faith and resolution. All of them were Gentiles. Whatever their background or their nationality, God included them in His plan and was working out His purposes through them. Jesus was to be the Saviour of the Gentiles as well as the Jews, of the outsiders as well as the insiders, of the broken, neglected and abused as well as the more conventional and less needy. God was preparing the way through these women to be the Saviour of the world.

To consider or discuss

• Jesus came from a very imperfect family line. How does that magnify the grace of God, and what hope does it give you concerning any disappointments you face in your family?

11 Dec

Thank God for taxes!

Bible reading Luke 2:1–3

It's not often we're grateful for taxes but here, at least, is one occasion when we should be. It was the need for the most powerful man in the world at the time, namely the ruler of the Roman empire, to collect taxes, and thus to have an accurate register of people on which to base his calculations, that led to Mary and Joseph being in Bethlehem just when they should have been at home in Nazareth.

The Caesar in question was Gaius Octavian, the grandnephew and adopted son of Julius Caesar. He had become sole ruler of Rome in 27 BC, when the title Augustus was conferred on him, and he was to be in power until AD 14. He presided over a period of great peace, enforced by the army, and left the empire with a commendable infrastructure of government, roads and communications. But that, of course, cost money; hence the need of the poll tax and the need to work out who should pay it. Elsewhere this census may have provided the Roman army with lists of conscripts, but the Jews had negotiated exemption from military service. Although Luke tells us the census took place all over the Roman world, he sharpens the focus of this general announcement and says that 'This was the first census that took place while Quirinius was governor of Syria' (v.2). He may state this to distinguish it from a second census which took place in AD 6 (mentioned in Acts 5:37).

The most ironic thing is that God used Caesar Augustus as a mere instrument in His hands. Augustus wouldn't have been aware of it. He would have thought he was taking his own decisions, acting independently, making up his own mind about a matter of fiscal policy. He wouldn't be manipulated by anyone! Yet, in truth, God was pulling his strings, just as He had done those of King Cyrus the Persian (Isa. 45:1–6) and a host of other rulers before him. The supreme ruler of the world was God, not Augustus. This census was the means by which God was going to accomplish the plan prepared centuries before. The child of Mary from Nazareth, who was destined to be the Messiah, had to be born in Bethlehem if Micah's prophecy (Micah 5:2) and all that it stood for was to come true. So one powerful ruler was unwittingly being used to cause another even more powerful ruler to be born in the right place so that people could recognise that the long-awaited successor to David, who was expected to be born in David's town, had come.

The reason this is ironic is that Augustus considered himself, and was considered by others, as virtually divine, if not actually a god (as some of his successors claimed). But even the tax system showed this to be highly suspect. There was only one God, the God whose prophet could foretell the future long in advance, and the God who could use an ordinary arrangement, such as the registration of the population and the administration of the tax system, to His glory.

Now there's preparation, and there's a reason to be thankful for taxes!

To consider or discuss

• As you think about the decisions of our world leaders, how far do you consider that God is at work, accomplishing His plan through them? Or do you think they are just human beings, acting on their own initiative, independent of God?

12 Dec

King Herod

Bible reading Matthew 2:1–18

The Christmas story is somewhat spoiled by the appearance of King Herod of Judea. True, Mary and Joseph couldn't find decent accommodation in Bethlehem, so Jesus was born in less-than-ideal surroundings. But even then there's a good side to the story: an innkeeper took pity on them and provided them with some shelter! But Herod? Is there anything good that could be said about him? Doesn't he spoil what might otherwise be a fairy-tale Christmas: you know, a young mum, a doting father, adoring shepherds, fleecy lambs and wonderful presents given by strangers? Isn't it a bit like an Al-Qaeda terrorist turning up at a Young Conservatives' ball?

Herod was a nasty piece of work. In today's reading he comes across as ignorant, insecure, devious and scheming. In real life he was worse than this. By the time Jesus was born he was an old man. Earlier in his life he had been a shrewd diplomat, a great builder and a generous benefactor, especially when Israel suffered a famine, but he wasn't now. He loved power, imposed heavy taxes on people and was consumed by paranoia. Any member of the family whom he suspected of conspiring against him was liquidated. One mother-in-law, one wife and three sons were on his hit list. He'd had ten wives and wrote six wills. The last will, written just four or five days before he died, divided his kingdom in three to ensure that no successor would be as powerful as he. On one occasion he'd executed a terrorist called Hezekiah without trial. And when the Jewish Council, known as the Sanhedrin, objected, he bided his time and then killed them too. You get the picture. Massacring the male infants of Bethlehem (vv.16–18) was entirely in character.

So, foreigners turning up at the palace and asking 'Where is the one who has been born king of the Jews?' may not have been the wisest thing these 'wise men' had ever done. Their enquiry would simply have fed Herod's suspicion and hastened his decline into a savage old age.

Why, then, is he allowed to spoil the story? Disturbing though it is, his presence testifies to the fact that Christ was born in the real world, not a fantasy world of tinsel, robins and cosy snow scenes. The world, then as now, was governed by greedy politicians who used force to protect their interests and augment their power. The world, then as now, was full of tragedy and pain, much of it man-made. Grief and sorrow had characterised the world ever since sin entered it, as the quotation about Rachel, from Jeremiah 31:15, reminds us. It was this real world that Christ was born to save.

King Herod the Great, the one we are thinking about here, died around the time of Jesus' birth, but his son and partial heir was to continue the family tradition of hostility to Jesus and conspired in the end with Pilate to have Him executed. Herod the Great sadly prepares the way for his son, Herod Antipas, to send Jesus to the cross. Like his father before him, and many rulers since, he tried to dispose of the One who alone was the legitimate ruler of the earth. Of course, they failed. But that didn't stop them trying.

To consider or discuss

- Who are the victims of oppression and injustice today? Pray for their deliverance and also for God to give us wise rulers who will govern with justice and righteousness.

13 Dec

What makes God laugh?

Bible reading Psalm 2

'How did you become a Christian?' I asked a young lady (we'll call her Sue) who had begun to come to church. 'Oh,' she replied, 'it was when I heard God laugh.' It wasn't your average reply! Sue explained that she was a nurse and one night on duty, all alone in the small hours at her workstation, thinking about some spiritual questions, she distinctly heard God gently laughing at her. In the circumstances God's laugh was an unmistakable signal of His love and care for her.

Some in the church objected when we sang a song that mentioned God laughing. For some reason they thought it irreverent! But Sue's testimony was hard to contradict. Moreover, Psalm 2:4 speaks about God laughing. This time, however, it's not the laughter of delight or affection but the laughter of scorn and derision. Just what is this psalm all about and how does it fit in with the Christmas story?

The psalm goes to the heart of the need for Christmas. The

nations have conspired to overthrow God's legitimate authority and eject Him as ruler of the world (vv.1–2). They regard Him as oppressive (v.3), and decide they can make a better job of ruling without Him. But their frenetic activity as they rush to join this alliance of evil simply reveals their folly. Do they really think they can run the world better than God? Do they really think they have the power, even when they have joined forces, to topple Him? Do they really think their rebellious action will have no consequences? They clearly believe the answer to all these questions is 'Yes'. But that only serves to expose them for the foolish leaders they are. No wonder God laughs at them (v.4).

Their way of ruling means God's honour is insulted, and He takes offence at their rebellion (v.5). Their form of government results in the wisdom of His law being overthrown, injustice being let loose, people being oppressed, and wickedness growing unchecked. His answer to the problems their rule causes is to put His own ruler in charge: one who is both a powerful King and a much loved Son (vv.6–7). If they are wise these world rulers will respect Him, rule according to His ways and recognise their accountability to Him. If they don't they will encounter His anger and face His judgment.

While this may seem to come from a very distant world, it really isn't so different from the one in which we live. Governments, presidents, prime ministers, kings, sultans and tyrants still behave in the way Psalm 2 warns against. Ordinary people still suffer the consequences of their unrighteous decisions and pay the price for their war-fuelled ambitions, as our newspapers and TVs tell us daily.

The birth of Jesus was the birth of God's much loved Son, who didn't seem very significant or powerful. He never led armies, mounted a military rebellion, seized a throne or engaged in tactics of shock and awe. Yet truly He was a baby born to be King, who through His perfect life, submissive death and astonishing resurrection would crush the powers of evil and restore the kingdom of God. As Isaiah said, 'He will not shout or cry out, or raise his voice in the streets. A bruised reed he will not break, and a smouldering wick he will not snuff out. [Yet] in faithfulness he *will* bring forth justice' (Isa. 42:2–4).

To consider or discuss

- Do we think of the birth of Christ on too small a scale? How far do we consider the political and international significance of His coming?

14 Dec

The bridge

Bible reading Luke 3:1–20

Today's reading takes us a little beyond the preparations that were made for the incarnation to the preparations made for the launch of Jesus' public ministry. John, of whom we'll learn more next week, was the advance party who published the news of the arrival of the Christ. He was an odd character who lived roughly, dressed simply, ate rustically and preached uncomfortably. But his message was crystal clear. Quoting Isaiah, he was the one who cried, 'Prepare the way for the Lord, make straight paths for him' (v.4).

Isaiah's evocative picture, the full version of which is in Isaiah 40:3–5, captures the way in which people would prepare the road ahead of the arrival of a royal guest. Hills and valleys would be levelled, potholes filled in and bends straightened out. To make sure the king's arrival was smooth and unimpeded, people would then build the ancient equivalent of a motorway. Even today we still tend to repaint things or lay fresh tarmac when royalty is expected, even if we don't go as far as levelling mountains! No one could mistake what John had in mind by way of the preparation required. He challenged his listeners to face up to the crisis of judgment (v.9) that their self-indulgent and dishonest lifestyles provoked (vv.10–14). They were to reject this way of living and show evidence of their change of direction (that's what repentance is) by being baptised in the River Jordan, where he was preaching. Far from being guilt-inducing fire and brimstone, John's preaching was 'good news' (v.18) because it told them how to get out of the spiritual hole into which they had fallen.

Expectations concerning the coming of the Messiah were already high at this time (v.15), and John's preaching did nothing to dampen them. People began to speculate if he himself was the Messiah. John categorically denied this. He was only the forerunner, pointing people to Jesus, who was the Christ.

Later, when John was in prison for offending King Herod by his straight talking, Jesus says of him, 'Among those born of women there is no-one greater than John; yet the one who is least in the kingdom of God is greater than he' (Luke 7:28). That's a curious thing to say. What could Jesus mean? Simply this. John was the greatest of men because he was the greatest and the last of the prophets, who was privileged to point out that, rather than being a distant dream, the age of the Messiah had dawned and the Person of the Messiah was among them. His message surpassed that of any previous prophet. And yet, though he lived to see the kingdom inaugurated, those who followed him would enter much more fully into its joy and privileges. He stood on the threshold; they stood firmly within. He pointed to the Messiah in faith; they pointed to the Messiah out of their experience. For him, the crucial events of the Messiah's life were still future, however imminent; for those who would follow, the events had happened and they had a deeper degree of certainty in their faith than was possible for John the Baptist.

John's role was crucial. He was the bridge who connected the old age and the new. But since we were born after the coming of Jesus, we live on the other side, in the new age. It's amazing to think that even the humblest believer in Christ is greater than John the Baptist.

To consider or discuss

• Read Luke 7:18–28. Do you think John the Baptist was disappointed by Jesus? How does Jesus answer his doubts? How does this help those who are uncertain about Jesus today?

For group discussion

This week's studies have led us to an appreciation of the preparation that God undertook down through the generations and among the world's rulers. Share your reactions to these studies. Did they reveal to you a God who relates both on a personal and on a more-than-personal level in the 'real' and institutional world of public affairs and politics?

1 To what extent do you believe that God is in control of the events and rulers of our world? Discuss what such a faith means in the light of the current news. Talk together about both your struggles with the idea and the evidences you see of God at work.

2 How does the inclusion of Herod in the narrative help us get a more realistic perspective of the Christmas story? How can we inject a greater degree of realism into our telling of the Christmas message and save it from suffocating under wrapping paper and too much Christmas pudding?

3 If you are able to, share something of your family histories and the way in which you can trace the goodness of God through them – goodness that has led to blessing on your families today.

4 What do you make of John the Baptist? What is there about him and his teaching that is relevant for the way we live as Christians now?

To guide your praying

'I urge, then, first of all, that requests, prayers, intercession and thanksgiving be made for everyone – for kings and all those in authority, that we may live peaceful and quiet lives in all godliness and holiness. This is good, and pleases God our Saviour ...' (1 Tim. 2:1–3).

Spend time this week praying for those who rule in our world, that God may grant the blessings mentioned in the verses above. Pray:

- for the leaders of the superpowers
- for our own prime minister and government
- for your local MP
- for the rulers of nations where Christians are persecuted.

Tell Out, My Soul, the Greatness of the Lord!

Preparing the way of the Lord ... among those most closely involved

In viewing the Christmas story, we change the focus again this week. The lens that can capture the distance and the wide-angle lens that can take in a broad panorama are now replaced by a lens that can take a close-up view. This week we look at the people God had prepared to play a particular role in the birth of the Messiah. Naturally, Joseph and Mary are the most prominent figures. But there are also Mary's relatives, Zechariah and his wife Elizabeth, whose role is to give birth to the one who is going to announce the Saviour's arrival, and Simeon and Anna, who've been longing for the Saviour to come. God has all the characters prepared and in place for the time when Jesus is to be born.

15 Dec

Zechariah

Bible reading Luke 1:5–25,67–79

If ever there was a day that didn't turn out as expected, it was the day Zechariah was on duty in the Temple. The priests weren't on duty all the time. They were divided into twenty-four groups and, apart from the major festivals when they were all called in, each group served in Jerusalem only two weeks a year. The turn of Abijah's section, to which Zechariah belonged, came round, and he found himself performing tasks he must have carried out many times before. No doubt he took his responsibilities seriously and served with care since he and his wife were devout and godly people. But, to be frank, it was the same old round of services and sacrifices – just the usual routine. The first hint of anything different was when he was chosen by lot to go into the Holy Place and offer incense rather than merely serving in the courtyards. He had no say in being chosen. God 'fixed it', as only God could, through the lot. It was an immense once-in-a-lifetime privilege but, even so, he was totally unprepared for what happened next. He may have been unprepared, but God wasn't.

Zechariah and Elizabeth come across as a pious, elderly couple of sweeties, yet there was an ache in their hearts since they were childless. In the most unexpected of places and the most unexpected way, God announced to Zechariah that their heartache was about to end. God's senior angel, Gabriel, was selected to deliver the news that they were to have a son. But he's to be no ordinary son. He would live an extraordinary life and fulfil an extraordinary mission. Not only was he to live as an alcohol-free Nazarite (see Numbers 6 for the background), but he was to be exceptionally blessed by the Holy Spirit to fill the role of Elijah, which Malachi had prophesied (remember the study of 7 December). The amazing thing is that the personal story of Zechariah and Elizabeth gets entangled with the wider story of Israel. Their son was to bring joy not only to them but to many others as well. No wonder Zechariah stumbled in believing the message. He might have needed warning that he was going to meet the angel Gabriel in the Temple that day, let alone warning of the good news Gabriel brought. Luke tells us, somewhat amusingly, that the crowds outside wondered what had happened as he took so long to reappear!

The rest, as they say, is history. Zechariah lost his voice, the son was born and, in due course, there was an argument about his name, which Zechariah settled when he miraculously rediscovered his voice. Having found his voice, he used it to praise God. Oh, and he composed a song that celebrated his son's special mission, using a bundle of Old Testament phrases and pictures, all of which focused on the salvation of God that he would herald.

It was hardly another routine day at the office! Zechariah was totally unprepared for it all – but God was in control, preparing the way for the birth of the one who would cry, 'Prepare the way for the Lord.'

To consider or discuss

- Can you think of a day when something totally unexpected happened? Looking back, can you see God's hand in it? Have you praised God for it? Since we 'do not even know what will happen tomorrow' (James 4:14), to what extent is your security in the God who providentially governs our lives?

16 Dec

Mary

Bible reading Luke 1:26–38

It's a totally absurd strategy. But that's the wonder of it. Imagine you had to plan an assault on an enemy-occupied country with a view to removing the enemies and installing a legitimate government that would bring freedom to the people in their homeland. How would you go about it? Sadly, recent history has plenty of examples to tell us how world powers normally go about such a task. Intelligence is gathered, strategies are carefully planned, armies are amassed, weapons deployed, terror is unleashed, and if all that proves superior to what the enemy can let loose in return, victory is assured.

Now contrast that with God's strategy. His rescue mission consisted of a teenage unmarried mum and her baby! But then, 'nothing is impossible with God' (v.37)! Here we focus on the mum and her learning of the role she was to play. We pick up quite a bit from Luke about her. We read of:

- *Her virginity.* The word used in Isaiah 7:14 means 'a young unmarried woman' rather than specifically a virgin. But Matthew leaves us in no doubt by using a more precise word which can only mean that Mary was a virgin when Jesus was born.
- *Her singularity.* God was not 'renting a womb'. The one who was to bear His Son in human form had to be a woman of exceptional character, and so she was. Everything about this report shows that. What distinguished her from others most, however, was that God had chosen her and had bestowed His favour on her.
- *Her perplexity.* Luke tells us she was 'greatly troubled' (v.29). Well, that's understandable. It's not every day an angel appears unannounced in your living room! It's bound to throw you a bit and make you wonder what's going on.
- *Her curiosity.* She recovers her composure enough to see that the message that Gabriel had brought raised more questions than it answered. How could she become a mother since she had not had sex with a man? She wasn't asking because she doubted God, but because she had an enquiring mind. God is more than capable of handling the questions we throw at Him.
- *Her humility.* When she receives a little more explanation, she displays a remarkable willingness to serve as an instrument by which God could achieve His purpose: 'May it be to me as you have said' (v.38). Her life was not her own; it was totally available for God to use as He chose. And what an honour she received as a result when she became the bearer of 'the Son of the Most High' who would occupy David's throne and whose kingdom would last for ever. We may pick and choose as to how God can use us, but it's always more rewarding to let Him have His way.

It really does seem that 'nothing is impossible with God'.

To consider or discuss

• Why do you think God put His plan for the salvation of the world in the hands of a young single mum and her baby? What can we learn from this of the ways God works? Maybe 1 Corinthians 1:18–31 is relevant to the incarnation as well as the cross.

17 Dec

Elizabeth

Bible reading Luke 1:23–25,39–45, 57–66

It's easy to miss Elizabeth in the Christmas story. She doesn't play a major part. Her scattered appearances cast her in a supporting role. Yet the drama would be much thinner without her.

We first meet her when she's playing a supporting role to her husband (vv.5–7). We learn she's from good stock, the priestly family of Aaron, and that, like Zechariah, she led a *devout life*. The sense is that they both loved God with all their hearts and loved their neighbours too. They not only observed all the ritual laws but lived clean lives and genuinely served others.

Yet, for all her piety, she nursed a *human sadness*. She was childless. In her day, this was more than a matter of personal or emotional sadness; childlessness was seen as a curse from God. People would have thought that for some reason these childless women had been disgraced by Him (see v.25). She's one of several barren women in Scripture, including Sarah and Hannah, whose childlessness was crucial for the revelation of God's miraculous and powerful grace. But before we jump to the happy ending too quickly, we should note that Elizabeth's devotion to God was no protection against her experiencing pain in life. It's a cruel myth that being a Christian, even a very committed one, guarantees a trouble-free, comfortable life. We still live in a fallen world and God, in His grace, often allows pain and suffering to occur so He can mould us to be more like Christ.

The next time we glimpse her (vv.23–25), she's received the good news that Zechariah brought back from Jerusalem and the child is on its way. I'm sure they were overjoyed, if not a little anxious at having a child at their age. But what's striking is the complete absence of self-centredness. Elizabeth expresses a *God-centred joy*, and testifies that it is the Lord who has caused her fertility. He wasn't required to. He wasn't answerable to her. It wasn't her 'right' to have a child, as many today believe. It was a mark of God's 'favour' that she was to become a mum.

In Elizabeth's third appearance (vv.39–45) she's playing a supportive role to Mary, who is also expecting. They have a remarkable conversation, inspired by the Holy Spirit. Given her age and somewhat surprising state, we might have expected the older woman to take centre stage and be the focus of attention. Convention would surely dictate that young (and unwed) Mary would show respect to her, but the conversation flows quite the other way round. Elizabeth displays great humility and not a whiff of jealousy. She demonstrates a *generous spirit* as she exalts the even greater news that Mary is going to be 'the mother of my Lord' (v.43).

Her last appearance is when John is born (vv.57–66) and an argument erupts over his name. Convention dictated that he would be named after one of the family, but she, since Zechariah is still for a moment or two unable to speak, insists he is to be called John, thus following Gabriel's instruction (v.13). It's wonderful to see this new, if somewhat mature, mum holding her own against family pressure and social convention. Here she demonstrates a *resolute mind*, determined to be obedient to God's will.

What an attractive woman this supporting actress was.

To consider or discuss

- Try to put yourself in Elizabeth's shoes. How would you have reacted to all that was going on? What can you learn from her?

18 Dec

Mary again

Bible reading Luke 1:46–56

Good news often makes us want to burst into song, but there's never been a better song than the one Mary sang while she was visiting Elizabeth. It's like a firework that explodes into the air and breaks into a multitude of dazzling colours. It is not exactly the song one might have expected because the baby doesn't actually rate a mention. Of course, the promise of the child is what lies behind the song, but the song is full of what God has done.

The song comes from deep within Mary's soul. It reminds us of the song Hannah sang on the birth of Samuel (1 Sam. 2:1–11), but it is marinated in all sorts of other Old Testament scriptures. Mary had no tools, such as the search facilities we have today, to help her compose such a song. What came from her was the result of long and prayerful meditation on the Scriptures. No wonder she 'found favour with God' (v.30).

Mary's personal story is entwined with the wider story of the people of Israel to whom she belonged. Her dream of the blessing of a child was matched by their dream of the blessing of freedom from oppression. And God was about to step in to make the dreams – hers and theirs – come true. The joy she feels is more than natural joy at the news that she's going to have a baby. It is joy that God is about to act.

He is a *mindful God* who has not ignored her plight (v.48), nor forgotten Israel's need (v.54). He remembers them because He is a holy God (v.49), and that means He always acts with integrity and is true to His word. He remembers that He gave His word in a covenant to Abraham, long ago (Gen. 12:1–3). Many times the covenant seemed threatened with extinction, or at least with being derailed because of Israel's sin. But now the covenant is being renewed.

He is a *merciful God*. When He does remember them, He doesn't do so in anger, frustration or with resentment, but with *mercy*. Mercy is what the undeserving need to help them out when they can't help themselves. God comes to rescue the humble and powerless, the hungry and poor, just as He did centuries before when the children of Israel were enslaved in Egypt. The prosperous and powerful don't need to be rescued – at least they don't think they do. There's only one condition to receiving God's mercy, and that's to 'fear him', to respect and reverence Him, rather than ignore Him or treat Him lightly (v.50).

Mary also celebrates the fact that He is a *mighty God*. He does not just have nice warm feelings towards the people of Israel, but the power to change their situation. Verses 51–53 picture God as a divine warrior, just as Psalm 24:8, Zephaniah 3:17, and a host of earlier scriptures had done. He defeats those who oppose Him and abuse their privileges by oppressing others. He has the power to reverse people's fortunes and to lift up the humble, feed the hungry and enrich the poor. And that's exactly what we see Him doing in Israel during the life of Mary's Son, and doing globally even more through His Spirit following His death and resurrection.

Mary doesn't prepare for the coming of Jesus by decorating the nursery and buying baby clothes and toys, but by praising God. She knows that her Son will be the One who rescues God's other son, Israel.

To consider or discuss

• If you were composing a song to celebrate the birth of Jesus, what would you include in it? Would it be anything like Mary's song?

19 Dec

Joseph

Bible reading Matthew 1:18–25

It takes a special kind of man to remain loyally in the background while all the attention centres on his wife. The Queen has Prince Philip, Mrs Thatcher had Denis and Mary had Joseph. At the nativity the spotlight is always on Mary, a young woman who had been especially prepared and chosen by God to bear His Son. (I remember my young son, who played Joseph in the church's nativity play one year, complaining that Mary got to sit down while he had to stand all the time!) Her soon-to-be husband, Joseph, receives only scant attention, and yet must have been as especially prepared and chosen as she was. He was indeed a special kind of man.

We know few facts about him except that he came from David's family line (v.20) and was a carpenter (Matt. 13:55). After the birth stories, he appears only twice in the Gospels: first, when he travels with Mary and Jesus for her presentation in the Temple (Luke 2:22–40), and second, when they took Jesus again to the Temple when he was 12 (Luke 2:41–52). The silence about him has led to the development of all sorts of traditions to fill the vacuum. Tradition, not unreasonably, suggests he was probably older than Mary since he doesn't figure much in the later story. It also suggests he was already a widower with children by the time he arranged to marry Mary.

Although we have little factual knowledge of Joseph, Matthew's brief portrait leaves us with a very strong impression of him. Joseph and Mary were 'pledged to be married' (v.18), which means a bit more than our modern idea of engagement. The pledge was binding, even though the marriage was still to come. Mary's pregnancy would have thrown a lesser man off balance, especially in a patriarchal society where all the cards were stacked in favour of men and against women, but not Joseph. Joseph handled this unique and uniquely challenging situation adeptly.

The way we handle crises usually reveals our true character, rather than being a case of us acting out of character. So it was with Joseph. He was a *righteous man* (v.19) who lived a clean life, seeking to conduct himself in the right way before God day after day. So when the news broke, he did not, to our knowledge, react with anger, resentment, disgust or censoriousness. It was his righteousness that led him to be a *compassionate man*. With great sensitivity to Mary, his first thought was to handle the situation discreetly rather than expose her to shame. But then a message from God revealed a third aspect of his character: he was a *spiritual man*. He was more than moral. There's a difference between being moral and being spiritual, as this incident illustrates. Joseph had no dramatic encounter with an angel when awake, but four times in his life (v.20; 2:13,19,22) God communicated with him in a dream, and he was alert enough to understand that God was directing him. So we discover that he was an *obedient man* as he acted upon the message he received from God. Finally, we see him as a *faithful man*, taking Mary home to live with him, yet not having sex with her until after Jesus was born, travelling to Bethlehem with her, and then escaping to Egypt with Mary and the baby before returning home to Nazareth (2:13–23).

Joseph's preparation was as important as Mary's; a different man could have wrecked the whole venture. What an engaging person Joseph is. How well he was prepared for his role.

To consider or discuss

• What do you make of Joseph? What qualities do you see in him that you would like to imitate? Pray for their development and list some practical steps you can take to cultivate them.

20 Dec

Simeon

Bible reading Luke 2:25–35

Every baby is special and every birth is significant. Even so, the birth of Jesus is in a class of its own. The significance was not that a baby was born, but who that baby was. The angels paved the way to understanding this was no ordinary baby. The manner in which others reacted, such as the shepherds and wise men (see next week's studies), suggests something extraordinary was happening. But there are two figures who appear when Mary, according to the custom (see Lev. 12), took her newborn child to Jerusalem for her purification. When they saw the child, they witnessed to His significance. Today we look at the man in the duo: Simeon.

Simeon, the person. Simeon led an exemplary life and was a model of faith, which showed itself not only by his attendance at the Temple but in an inner longing he felt. His life revolved around an unfilled spiritual hunger. Day after day he had asked God to rescue Israel from oppression and restore the people to freedom under the reign of God Himself – what Luke calls 'the consolation of Israel' (v.25). He didn't let up, and he didn't give up. He patiently waited until God would answer his prayer. Furthermore, Luke tells us that Simeon was sensitive to the Holy Spirit's ministry in his life. He received an assurance from the Holy Spirit – an assurance others probably questioned – that his hopes would be fulfilled during his lifetime, but he still remained sensitive to the daily guidance of the Spirit. So, 'moved by the Spirit' (v.27), he went into the Temple courts on the very day Mary and Joseph came to Jerusalem for her presentation.

Simeon, the worshipper. That special day, Simeon's prayers were answered, his hopes realised, his waiting rewarded, and the promise fulfilled. When Simeon took Jesus in his arms, he wasn't doing so as a grandfather admiring any young baby and the miraculous mystery of new life. He was seeing past the usual joy and exhibiting a deeper reaction than the normal human emotion engendered by a birth. This child proved that God had kept His word, to him personally and to His covenant people as a whole. 'The consolation of Israel' had come. Simeon responds, not by praising the parents, but by praising God. That day he worshipped more deeply and with greater thankfulness than he'd ever done before. When God answered his prayers, he praised God. How often do we receive something from God but express thanks to others rather than to God, or even go about our other business and forget to praise Him at all?

Simeon, the prophet. Then Simeon said some remarkable things about the destiny of the child he held in his arms. Positively, this child would bring about salvation for Israel (vv.30–31) and revelation to the Gentiles (v.32). His ministry wouldn't be confined to rescuing Israel but would include bringing the despised Gentiles in to God's kingdom as well. Negatively, this salvation would not be without cost. It would necessarily result in the overthrow of those who resisted Him as they fell under His judgment (v.34). And it would cost His mother dearly too (v.35). She would see a spear pierce her Son's body as He was crucified just outside the city where they were hearing these wonderful things said about Him. As the spear entered Him, so a sword of grief and pain would enter her heart as she watched Him unjustly condemned and so cruelly executed.

To consider or discuss

• 'Blessed are those who hunger and thirst for righteousness ...' (Matt. 5:6). How spiritually hungry are you? Do you long for more of God in your life or are you already full with other things?

21 Dec

Anna

Bible reading Luke 2:36–38

I wonder if you've ever been to a party and been surprised to find there someone you didn't expect to see. You may just have stopped yourself asking, 'What are they doing here?', even though you thought it. I suspect that's how many of us treat Anna – one of the curiosities who creeps unannounced on to the stage when the infant Jesus was 'presented' in the Temple.

Who was this woman? Luke tells us a surprising amount about her.

• She was 'a prophet'. Luke shows no embarrassment in saying that this woman was a prophet. She stood in the long line of women in Israel who were inspired by the Holy Spirit as prophets, including Miriam, Deborah, Huldah and Isaiah's wife. God had often spoken through women in the past, and was doing so now through her.
• She was 'the daughter of Phanuel', although sadly we know nothing about him.
• She was 'of the tribe of Asher'. Asher was one of the northern tribes which existed on the margins of Israel, and an insignificant

one at that. After the Exile these tribes were dispersed and mostly disappear into oblivion. But Anna turns up in the infancy story to represent them. Unlike Simeon, she wasn't a native of Jerusalem, but had returned there from the dispersion. Her part in the story is highly significant. You might expect a woman from the pure southern tribes to be in Jerusalem, but she's from the margins, drawn to Jerusalem in the hope of finding a Saviour. She represents those who don't quite belong, indicating the scope of salvation.

- She was widowed. Indeed, like a number of war widows I've known, she'd been married for only a short time and widowed a very long time. She must have often felt lonely and deserted, especially in days when having a husband was almost the only dignified way for a woman to support herself. But God had not forgotten her.
- She was old. She was 84. But what a ministry she had, as many elderly people still do.
- She was devoted. She 'never left the temple', gave herself to prayer and to keeping the expectation of the Messiah alive. She held on to God's promises when others had given up. What patience!
- She was sensitive to the Spirit's revelation. She must have witnessed hundreds of similar family occasions over the years, but her spiritual sight was still sharp, and she could spot the one she'd been looking for and identified Jesus as the Messiah. Her natural reaction was to thank God.
- She was chatty. You can just imagine her, can't you? An elderly woman who wouldn't stop chatting! She probably badgered any number of visitors to the Temple, some of whom might well have thought she was a bit dotty, but that didn't stop her from telling everyone that the One who would redeem Israel had arrived. If they took her seriously at all, they may have looked for a powerful leader, but a baby! Who'd have thought it? Well, Anna did – and she was right.

Anna may be one of the curiosities of the gospel, a woman we may be tempted to write off as insignificant. But I'm glad she's there. She is far from insignificant.

To consider or discuss

• What can I learn from the example of Anna? How does Anna's story affect my attitude to elderly Christians whom I might be tempted to regard as insignificant?

For group discussion

This week's studies took us 'up-close and personal' as we looked at Zechariah, Mary, Elizabeth, Joseph, Simeon and Anna. Did you find it easier to identify with these studies than the previous ones that concerned the grander scale of things? Or did they seem just another part of the mosaic that reveals the full Christmas story?

1 Share your reactions to the characters in this week's readings. Do they come across to you as real human beings or as premier league saints, untroubled by the shortcomings of ordinary people like you and me? Which character do you identify with most, and why?

2 Which is your favourite character from this week's readings, and why? What spiritual lessons have you learned from him or her?

3 How should we treat Mary? If some value her too highly, others value her insufficiently. What is the right way to think of a woman whom God favoured so highly?

4 Do Simeon and Anna teach us that we are sometimes too impatient for God to act? What can we learn from them about 'waiting on God'?

To guide your praying

Each take one of the characters in the Christmas story and:
- find one specific thing about them for which to thank God
- identify one way in which they are an example to you
- ask what one lesson you can learn from them
- or single out a truth they teach you.

Then turn those discoveries into a conversation with God.

Christians Awake! Salute the Happy Morn

Preparing the way of the Lord ... in our own lives

School nativity plays normally end up with a pretty crowded stage as Mary and Joseph become successively smothered by the innkeeper and his wife, the shepherds and their accompanying sheep, and the wise men and their gifts. So far we've not mentioned them, but during Christmas week we look at their part in the story, not only to discover what the Bible actually says about them rather than what subsequent traditions and imaginative playwrights have claimed, but also to discover something of their inner motives and attitudes. These serve as an example to us and will guide us as we prepare ourselves spiritually to 'salute the happy morn'.

22 Dec

Receiving

Bible reading Luke 2:7; John 1:10–13

The poor innkeeper tends to get a rough ride when the Christmas story is told every year, but I think he is misunderstood. 'What, no room for a pregnant young mum who is clearly about to give birth? How unfeeling! Surely he could have found a room.' Well, he did, even if it meant sharing the space with the animals. The innkeeper received the young couple as best he could.

So many myths have grown up around Luke's words. We're not to think of this as a commercial inn running out of rooms (after all, there were many visitors in town for the census) and putting the young couple up in the stable (one worse than sleeping in the garage would be today). Luke doesn't use the word for a commercial inn, so he's probably referring to a private house where the guestroom was already occupied. Mary and Joseph could use the common family space where everything happened, and which people freely shared in those days with their animals. Then it was normal to find an animal's feeding trough in such a room, either as a wooden stall or built into the floor. When a birth took place, the men were turfed outside and the village midwife came to superintend the delivery. Once born, the baby would have been placed on fresh straw in the feeding trough.

At least these hosts offered some shelter. They received the couple and made space for the arrival of baby Jesus and, no doubt, joined in the festivities that followed. If the criticism of these hosts is unjust, John tells us this criticism can be justly directed elsewhere. Not everyone welcomed Him or made space for Him in their lives – even those who might have been most likely to do so. He created people, but when He came to His creatures they didn't recognise Him. More particularly, He came to God's specially elect people, but on the whole they didn't recognise this special Son of God either. He came to bring light to a dark world, but rather than welcoming it as one might have expected, people found it strange and tried again and again to snuff it out (John 1:9). They preferred the familiar darkness because it cloaked their sinful lives (John 3:19).

The few who did receive Him, however, inevitably received the wonderful gift He brought with Him. They not only benefited from His presence and His wisdom, but also from His power to make a difference for them. Receiving Him meant that He removed the separation between them and their God, and cured the family rift that was caused by sin. He gave them 'the right to become children of God' (John 1:12); to be adopted back into God's family, with all the obstacles removed. They found out what it really meant to be created by God as they became more than creatures and became children.

What is involved in receiving Jesus? John explains that to receive Him is to believe in Him. To believe is more than to accept He existed or mentally assent to His teaching. It means to trust Him with your life, to obey His words and enjoy His gift of eternal life. We spend a lot of time preparing to receive visitors at Christmas. Let's not ignore the need to receive Jesus as well. Even those for whom belief is their life-stance need to receive Him by intentionally making space for Him in a busy Christmas.

To consider or discuss

- In what sense have you received Jesus, and how are you planning to do so this Christmas?

23 Dec

Singing

Bible reading Luke 2:8–14

If we were to play the TV game *Family Fortunes* and ask contestants to name what the greatest number of people mention when asked to think of something associated with Christmas, I guess after 'children' and 'families' would come 'music'. Think of the race to release an album or top the chart with a single at Christmas.

Christmas carols are a greatly appreciated Christmas tradition, even among those who don't usually sing! People often trace the origin of modern Christmas carols back to the mid-eighteenth century, but surely their true origin is found in that first Christmas. When the angel announces Jesus' conception to Mary, she sings. When Zechariah witnesses the birth of his son, John, he sings. It's what we naturally do when we've something to celebrate. There's no better way to express our emotion. Why, even the most hardened man, who'd never normally be seen dead singing, does so when his football team wins the cup!

When Jesus was born, the climax of the singing was reached when the angelic choir burst on to the scene, set the night sky ablaze and hearts racing as they awakened the earth to the news of His birth and sang, 'Glory to God in the highest, and on earth peace to those on whom his favour rests' (v.14).

Truth to tell, carols contain some wonderful words, but they also contain some curious ones that don't quite make sense to us now, even if they did once. Some of them refer to past customs we've forgotten all about. But most are great and we can immediately understand their message. Let's ask exactly what the words of the angels' carol mean. The art of poetry or hymn writing is to express thoughts and images extremely concisely, and that's certainly true of the angels' song. So let's put it in different words and expand them a bit to help us understand them: 'To God be the glory, the God, that is, who lives in the highest heaven, at the pinnacle of our universe. In spite of His distant majesty, this God is anything but remote and has intervened on earth and given us the good news of His gift of a Saviour, the Messiah (v.11). As a result of His birth may there be true peace and justice on earth, a peace that can be experienced not just by troubled Israel but, through Israel, by people of any race on whom God settles His grace and favour.' Wow! That's a cause for celebration worth turning into song.

Ever since then, the world has done its best to continue in conflict and to ensure the noise of battle and injustice drowns out the good news the angels sang. But the song will not be silenced. The message goes on being celebrated. And where people take it seriously and turn to the Saviour, the peace they sang about is experienced and transforms the lives of individuals, families and communities. No wonder Christmas is a time to sing.

To consider or discuss

- Listen to some Christmas music, or at the very least sing through (or, if you must, read through!) a favourite carol or two. What do the words tell you about the incarnation, and how do they help you to express joy at the birth of Jesus?

24 Dec

Seeking

Bible Reading Matthew 2:1–10

I'm probably a sad case, but I don't enjoy TV quiz or game shows, whereas I do enjoy programmes such as *CSI* and other detective dramas. It always seems to me the former are designed to make sure people fail and even suffer humiliation – the title *Weakest Link* says it all – whereas the latter are designed to succeed. It's the seeking for truth, it's the desire to find out who did it or what really happened that appeals to me, even if the end result is somewhat predictable, even cheesy. *CSI* and the like are about seekers in search of truth, and determined seekers usually find what they are looking for.

The mysterious wise men who came 'from the east' (v.1), and who go under the strange name of 'Magi', were genuine seekers. Tradition says they were three kings, but that tells us more than Matthew does. The eastern land from which they came was Arabia, the land beyond the Jordanian deserts. The gifts they brought were all typical of that region. Magi were originally a priestly caste in Persia, but the term was later used generally of magicians and astrologers. Astrology had

developed into quite a science and was thought to provide clues
to the questions of life. So these seekers fit the picture. They were
not, though, disinterested scientists. Once they detected some clues
they followed where they led as passionately as any TV detective
follows the evidence. Most English translations may make you think
they were doing no such thing. If they 'saw his star in the east' (v.2)
shouldn't they have gone east in search of the king? The conundrum
is easily solved. What the text actually says is that they saw the star
at its rising (that is, in the east) and then followed it.

Today we're interested in identifying the star in the light of
modern astronomy. The Magi weren't concerned to explain it by
discovering whether or not it was a comet, a nova or a conjunction
of planets. To them, the star had a deeper meaning. It meant a new
and special king was born to the Jewish people, one whose birth
deserved to be marked by making a journey to pay Him homage.

Their quest leads them roughly in the right direction, but only
roughly. They don't have all the clues they need to find the baby
immediately. As in all the best detective stories, working on what
they have leads them on a bit of a false trail to start with. They
piece things together and naturally conclude that if it's a king that's
being born he'll be born in a palace. So they head off to Herod's
palace. But that's because they're missing a vital piece of evidence,
namely the prophecy of Micah (Micah 5). They needed to add to
their human logic the divine revelation of Scripture. If they'd had
that originally they might have gone straight to Bethlehem. Refusing
to be put off, the wise men follow the fresh clues they were given
(v.6), and carry on their search for the king until at last they found
him when the star came to a halt 'over the place where the child
was' (v.9). Interestingly, Herod's advisers have the same information
but don't follow up on it because they don't have the spiritual hunger
that makes them seekers.

Our culture encourages us to look for easy answers, and we're
often impatient if we can't get them quickly. But most worthwhile
quests in life, whether in science, criminal investigation or the quest
for personal fulfilment, demand perseverance and determination.
Spiritually, the answers aren't always easy, but they're always worth
the quest because seekers find (Matt. 7:7–12).

To consider or discuss

- Have you followed the evidence about Jesus carefully, or do you expect easy answers from God in your spiritual life? Have you been tempted to turn aside after the slightest difficulty, or are you a determined seeker?

25 Dec

Worshipping

Bible reading Matthew 2:11

Happy Christmas! This Christmas day we journey a little further with the wise men. Admirers often coo over a newborn baby and say, 'She's gorgeous' or 'He's adorable.' Sometime later when the wise men reached their destination 'they saw the child with His mother Mary, and they bowed down and worshipped'. This was much more than saying, 'Isn't he adorable?' Although the word 'worship' can simply mean to show respect to a human leader, the fact that they bowed down in obeisance to Him, combined with the way in which Matthew uses the word 'worship', suggests this was more than mere respect. It was to bow down in homage and to express personal recognition of His kingship and open-ended submission to His authority.

Why the Magi should have been so excited about the birth of a new 'king of the Jews' is puzzling. Why did it concern them? It's puzzling unless they saw this king as being a king for more than the Jews alone and as a ruler who would prove beneficial to the whole world. The fact of their visit, and their behaviour and gifts on arrival, suggest they did. Probably this is Matthew's real point in including them in the Christmas story. All the others who crowd the stage at the nativity were Jews, even if some of them, like Anna, were somewhat marginalised, and others, like the shepherds, somewhat suspect. But the Magi were Arabs and therefore Gentiles. They came from right outside the predictable social network to worship Jesus.

Matthew is acutely sensitive to the way in which from the moment the angels announced Jesus' birth, He fulfils the Old Testament Scriptures. He's keen on pointing out the connections. Several of those scriptures looked forward to the Messianic age, when Gentiles would come and worship the God-given king. Psalm 72:10–11, for example, had predicted that 'the kings of Tarshish and of distant shores will bring tribute to him; the kings of Sheba and Seba will present him gifts. All kings will bow down to him and all nations will serve him.' Isaiah 60:3 had promised, 'Nations will come to your light, and kings to the brightness of your dawn', and then verse 6 had mentioned gold and incense, or frankincense, as gifts they'd bring with them. Foreigners would have a place in this new kingdom, and the wealth of nations, Isaiah claims (Isa. 60:11–12), would be brought to the One whose kingdom would triumph over all others.

Coincidence? I think not. The Magi were not casual visitors who happened to drop by, but genuine worshippers who had travelled from a distant land to pay homage. Matthew joins up the dots and sees the Magi's coming as fulfilling those ancient prophecies. The promised light, he rightly concludes, shone not from Jerusalem, or even an unnamed king, but from a house in Bethlehem and the baby who was born there, whose name was Jesus. Truly, the universal King who would rule with justice had come.

His arrival deserved more than mere admiration and the expression of how adorable the baby was. It demanded then, and demands now, nothing less than submission and reverent obeisance.

To consider or discuss

- Read Psalm 72 or Isaiah 60:1–11. How do they enhance your understanding of Christ's rule? Do they lead you not just to admire but to worship the baby of Bethlehem?

26 Dec

Giving

Bible reading Matthew 2:11

Boxing Day was originally the day when rich people gave their servants a box containing a present to open, though few families wait until Boxing Day before opening their presents now. A great deal of our preparation for Christmas is to do with presents. Unless you're particularly imaginative, you probably go through nightmares working out what you can buy, trying to avoid giving the same old present again or the unwanted gift that will be recycled next year!

Although many nativity plays suggest the shepherds donated a sheep or two to baby Jesus, they almost certainly didn't. The sheep weren't theirs to give. If the shepherds were working out on the Bethlehem hills, the sheep were probably marked for slaughter as Temple sacrifices. And what would the young couple have done with the lambs, so far from home? The biblical precedent comes rather from the wise men who 'opened their treasures and presented him with gifts of gold and of incense and of myrrh'.

They must have thought about their gifts before they left their home in modern-day Iran and carried them all those miles to Bethlehem. The gifts proved to be extraordinarily appropriate. They were hugely symbolic, although the wise men probably didn't realise that at the time since they were typical products of their area. Gold was a gift suitable for a king, frankincense was a suitable gift for a priest, and myrrh was a spice that, because it was used in burials, pointed forward to Jesus' death.

The wise men have set us a tremendous example. When wondering about the presents we give to family and friends, do we ever stop to think about the present we can bring to Jesus, or do we count going to church at Christmas time as present enough? Where does He figure in our plans and preparations?

There must be, as it were, many things on Christ's present list! One thing that would delight Him is the giving of a present to those who don't have much financial support. While we may struggle to think of what we can give to those who seemingly already have everything, there are plenty of others who live just down the road, as well as people on the other side of the world, who don't know where the means to survive tomorrow is going to come from. So why not donate to a homeless project, cook a meal for the lonely, fill a shoe box full of goodies for someone in need, or send a financial gift to a development or disaster relief organisation? Jesus might say, 'Whatever you did for one of the least of these ... you did for me' (Matt. 25:40).

Sometimes, however, that can be the easy option. Maybe there's another present we need to give to Jesus Himself – a present which consists of surrendering our lives to Him as Lord; fulfilling a promise made earlier in the year but long-forgotten; obeying His call to a particular form of service; or deciding to tithe our income regularly. As Christina Rossetti's carol puts it:

> *What can I give Him,*
> *Poor as I am?*
> *If I were a shepherd,*
> *I would bring a lamb;*
> *If I were a wise man,*
> *I would do my part;*
> *Yet what I can I give Him –*
> *Give my heart.*

To consider or discuss

- What's on your present list for Jesus this year?

27 Dec

Speaking

Bible reading Luke 2:15–20

Usually we can't suppress our urge to tell others good news, whether they want to hear it or not. When there's a new arrival in our family, we don't ask permission of our friends and neighbours; we blurt out, 'She's had a girl!' or 'I've just become a grandfather. It was a boy!' Similarly, when our favourite team is winning, or the local team has just been promoted, we gossip the good news quite naturally. When, with the encouragement of the angels, the shepherds visited the baby Jesus, they were not only full to overflowing with praise to God but irrepressible in spreading the good news of the Saviour's birth to others.

Nothing very remarkable about that, you might think, and at one level you might be right. But at another level there is something quite remarkable about it. We've a fairly romantic image of the shepherds: they were strong and rugged guys used to cold hillsides and fighting off wild beasts who attacked their flocks, but guys who actually had tender hearts for their fleecy sheep. The truth is a little different. True, they were rugged guys used to the cold, the loneliness and the danger the job involved, but that made them hard men. How much they truly cared for their sheep is questionable. Their job put them outside the normal run of community life and unable to join in the routine of religious life. This made people suspicious of them and they were assumed to be dishonest. You never bought anything from a shepherd because it was bound to be stolen. Shepherding was on a list of despised occupations, and a shepherd's witness was not accepted in a law court.

Given this, it's somewhat remarkable that God chose the shepherds to be the first evangelists to spread the good news of the Saviour's birth. Yet surprising though it may seem, it fits the picture of the way God works. The first people to learn the good news, even before the baby's birth, were the women Mary and Elizabeth. Their testimony wouldn't have counted for much either in official, male-dominated circles. God consistently uses the ordinary people, even nobodies, to spread the good news, perhaps because their words have a ring of truth about them that is often lacking when religious professionals, paid to say predictable religious things, speak.

Still today, the best messengers of the good news of Christ are ordinary men and women who, like the shepherds, gossip quite naturally about what they have witnessed of God's love. It doesn't require ordination, or a theology degree, or an ability to argue convincingly against Richard Dawkins to speak of Jesus effectively. It takes an experience of Jesus, such as the shepherds had. It takes enthusiasm, which the shepherds demonstrated. No one is going to be convinced that Jesus is good news if His followers are boring, inhibited or holier-than-thou-type characters. It also takes courage. People must have thought the shepherds mad. Hard men like shepherds don't usually have a religious experience, such as seeing a choir of angels in the sky. And they certainly don't usually get excited over a baby! But that didn't stop them from saying what they'd seen. The courage needed in a secular society may be different from the courage they needed in a more religious climate, but it still takes guts to speak of Jesus. But then, we don't normally have difficulty passing on good news, so why hold back passing on the good news of Jesus?

To consider or discuss

• When did you last speak to someone about the good news of Jesus? If it's been some time, ask yourself 'Why?' What opportunities do you have this Christmas to speak about Him?

Understanding

Bible reading Luke 2:19; John 1:14

Facts are one thing, what they mean quite another. We don't just repeat details of events, we try to make sense of them and explain them. The birth of Jesus certainly required some explaining if its significance for the world was to be grasped. The two verses we're looking at today touch on the way Mary and then the disciples sought to understand Christmas.

With all the strange happenings that occurred when Jesus was born, Mary might have been forgiven if her thoughts were in a whirl of confusion. But rather than letting her mind race, she 'treasured up all these things and pondered them in her heart'. The impression of her as a reflective person, already gained from her submissive reply to the angel's announcement in Luke 1:38, is reinforced here.

She doesn't panic or go to pieces, but nor does she float across the surface of things, refusing to allow them to affect her. She internalises them, quietly seeking to piece the meaning and implications of things together. She knew the circumstances of her Son's conception and birth were far from usual. She'd been told her child was not only special, but unique. She'd been informed He was to be the means by which many would be rescued from sin and oppression. She'd begun to see just how special He was when manly shepherds came to pay homage. Later His uniqueness became even more apparent when men from distant eastern lands came to visit her, and when Simeon spoke a blessing over her. But how would it work out? What were the implications for her, especially in view of Simeon's ominous words about a sword piercing her own soul (Luke 2:35)? As her Son grew, there were more puzzling matters to ponder, for instance, after He visited the Temple as a 12-year-old (Luke 2:51).

It would be years before the pieces of the jigsaw fell into place and the picture made sense. When it did, the picture was at first a painful one as she saw her Son executed. But then she encountered Him alive again a few days later. All the time, though, she kept thinking, meditating, and no doubt asking God to make sense of it all.

In John 1:14 we see the sense the disciples made of Jesus' life once they were able to bring some perspective to it. Having listened to His teaching for years, seen His miracles and reactions to people, as well as how He endured the irrational hostility He seemed to provoke from the authorities, they could draw only one conclusion. This man was God Himself living among them as a human being; the Creator residing among them as a creature; the Word transformed into human flesh. He brought light to a world of darkness; radiated glory in a world of shame; personified truth in a world of lies; modelled integrity in a world of fakes; and embodied God's grace in a world where there was little mercy but much 'ungrace'. Their understanding was that God had revealed Himself to them in Jesus, not as a flash in the pan, but as One who lived among them long enough to be unmasked as a fraud if that was what He was. But they couldn't fault Him. They could only conclude that He was the 'I am' (John 8:58), the 'Son of God' (Matt. 16:16), the 'way and the truth and the life' (John 14:6). The only response that made sense was to believe in Him.

Christmas is a big event. We'll never fathom the explanation for it completely, but that doesn't mean we shouldn't start to do so, just as Mary and the disciples did.

To consider or discuss

- 'Love the Lord your God … with all your mind' (Mark 12:30).
  How much is yours a thinking faith, seeking understanding of the meaning of the gospel? What sense have you made of the events of Christmas this year?

For group discussion

This week's studies have introduced us to the reactions of others to the Christmas story – the people of Israel in general, Jesus' mother in particular, but also angels, shepherds and the wise men. Who do you relate to most easily? Which of them expressed your own reaction to the Christmas story? And which reaction least expresses your reaction? Why do you think that is?

1 Read Luke 2:8–20. Why do you think God chose shepherds to hear the good news? Why do you think God sent an angel as His messenger? How did they recognise him? Are you aware of angelic messengers visiting our world today? Have you any stories you can share about their activities? What is the significance of the message he brought in verse 11, and how does the song the choir sang in verse 14 relate to our world? In what ways can the shepherds serve as examples to us?

2 Share your favourite carol with each other and explain what it means to you.

3 What do you struggle with in the Christmas story? What do you find it hard to believe or to make sense of? Share your difficulties with each other and see if a member of your group can shed light on them.

4 Look back on this week's studies and identify a key action point from them to build on in the new year.

To guide your praying

This week, of all weeks, it would be good to focus our prayers on adoration. Here is an ancient prayer of adoration by Bernard, Abbot of Clairvaux (1090–1153), which is probably the basis for the hymn 'Jesus, the very thought of You':

Jesus, how sweet is the very thought of You!
You fill my heart with joy.
The sweetness of Your love surpasses the sweetness of honey.
Nothing sweeter than You can be described; no words can
express the joy of Your love.
Only those who have tasted Your love for themselves can
comprehend it.

*In Your love You listen to all my prayers, even when my wishes
are childish, my words confused, and my thoughts foolish.
And You answer my prayers, not according to my own
misdirected desires, which would bring only bitter misery, but
according to my real needs, which brings me sweet joy.
Thank You, Jesus, for giving Yourself to me. Amen.*

O Come,
O Come, Immanuel

Preparing the way of the Lord ...
for His coming again

Advent proper is not only a way of preparing for the first coming of Christ but also for His second coming. As is evident in so many of the New Testament writings, the early Christians pulsated with the hope of Christ's return. In the remaining days we look at three key passages and three key themes connected with the second coming.

29 Dec

Hoping

Bible reading 2 Peter 3:1–14

No teaching about the second coming is so realistic, and so scary, as Peter's writing in his second letter. Like a musical chord, Peter sounds four notes that make for a wonderful harmony here.

The first note is that of *expectation* (vv.3–4). Christians are not to be surprised when cynics pour scorn on the idea of Christ's return. People, Peter teaches, will mock the idea throughout the 'last days', by which he means the whole period from the Day of Pentecost to the second coming. The Church, then, can always expect the idea to be ridiculed. Peter reveals that people have an ulterior motive for doing so. They don't want to face God because they'd prefer to live life as if they're unaccountable to anyone and anything but their own desires.

The second note is that of *explanation* (vv.5–9). The sceptics say we are foolish to hold on to the belief since it's taking such a long time to be fulfilled and nothing ever changes. But Peter gives three reasons why we can still believe: (1) It's not true that nothing ever changes. Think back to the creation and the Flood. Things certainly changed then! The closing decades of the twentieth century were full of surprises. It's foolish to think the future is trapped in an endless cycle of the expected; (2) God doesn't calculate time in the way we do. He exists in eternity, not time; (3) God's delay is motivated by His patient love since He does not want anyone to perish.

The third note is that of *exploration* (vv.10–13). What will the day of Christ's return be like? (1) As the New Testament constantly teaches, it will be unexpected; (2) It will be total in its impact. The whole of creation will be caught up in it. There will be no spectators, only participants. 'Everything in it will be laid bare' (v.10) means that just as a fire can cause a wall of a house to collapse, revealing the interior, so all the secrets of our lives will be disclosed; (3) In apocalyptic and scary terms, Peter describes the destruction of the creation as we know it. It misses the point to speculate whether or not he's describing a nuclear explosion. He's using imagery which takes account of God's promise to Noah not to destroy the earth by water again (Gen. 9:11); (4) But don't miss his real point. This destruction of the old order is the first step towards the renewal of creation, the making of a new heaven and earth, which will be 'the home of righteousness' (v.13). So destruction may be a reality but it is not the finality. It's a means to recreation.

The fourth note is that of *exhortation* (vv.11,14). This is Peter's real burden. Since our destination is the recreated 'home of righteousness', we ought to get in practice for living there now. Just as we might learn a foreign language before a move overseas, so we should be learning the lifestyle of the new creation now. And just as we wouldn't dream of running a marathon without training, so we shouldn't think of entering the renewed creation without training for it. This means living holy lives now, and aiming for lives that are in total harmony with God.

Peter's message is 'Get in training!'

To consider or discuss

• Many look after themselves with an exercise regime or a dietary plan. Jot down an outline of your exercise regime to prepare you for living in the new creation.

30 Dec

Purifying

Bible Reading 1 John 2:28–3:10

There's all the difference in the world between the apprehension or fear a child might know when threatened with the appearance of their father or headmaster after they've done something wrong and the excitement of a little child who is longing for their grandparents, laden with presents and full of goodwill, to appear for Christmas. John uses the phrase 'when he appears' twice (2:28; 3:2), and both times speaks of looking forward to the second coming as a welcome event, like the coming of the grandparents.

Surely no one can miss the upbeat tone in these verses. John believes it is possible to be 'confident and unashamed' (2:28) at the coming again of Christ. There's no great secret to such confidence. It arises out of doing more of the same or, as John puts it, from 'continu[ing] in him'. So we don't need to discover some mystery plan. We need to go on believing, go on loving, go on confessing sin, go on taking our stand on the truth – these are the great themes of John's letter – if we want such confidence. Some of us, though, may not feel confident. How can John be so sure? He expands his thinking in the verses that follow.

First, we can be confident because of *who we are* (3:1). We're greatly loved children of God who have a secure relationship with our Father already. The relationship doesn't depend on us but on the love which He 'has lavished on us' (3:1). Others may not appreciate who we are, any more than we always appreciate other people's children! But that makes no difference. Being a child of God is not something we aspire to but something we already are because of grace.

Second, we can be confident because of *what we will be* (3:2). True, our loving Father must often be disappointed in us, but His love is unshaken because He knows what the future holds. When Christ returns we will be transformed into His likeness. The image of God in us, currently marred by sin, will be fully restored and we'll reflect the Christ into whose face we gaze. That day will bring about the completion of Christ's work in us. Paul says something very similar in Philippians 1:6: 'He who began a good work in you will bring it to completion at the day of Jesus Christ' (RSV).

Third, we can be confident if we do *what we should do* (3:3). The hope of being transformed should not lead us to spiritual indolence – 'He'll change us one day, so why bother making any effort now?' – but to spiritual inspiration. It should lead us to redouble our efforts to be like Him now. Since 'he is pure', we too should live pure lives, as free from sin as possible. The rest of today's reading expands on what is involved in living a pure life.

Waiting for the second coming is never about passive resignation but always about active preparation. Hoping for this future return leads to purifying in this present life.

To consider or discuss

• Look back on this year and identify elements of which you are ashamed, or which cause you to lack confidence 'at His appearing'. What steps can you take to purify yourself?

31 Dec

Waiting

Bible reading Titus 2:11–14

My wife and I are trying to cultivate the art of being late! We know it's not polite to turn up for a dinner party too early, but somehow we always manage to do so. When we're expecting people, unless they arrive five minutes before time we think they're late! As you can guess, we don't find waiting easy! Yet waiting is what we're currently called to do as Christians!

But there's waiting and there's waiting, and a couple of things make the difference between them.

The first is *what we're waiting for.* Waiting for the dentist or for confirmation of bad news is very different from looking forward to a joyful occasion. We say about the former, 'I can't wait to get it over with'; we say about the latter, 'We can't wait for it to happen.' For believers, the second coming of Christ is an event about which we should be saying, 'I can't wait for it to happen.' We should anticipate it keenly because of the joy it will bring. See how Paul describes it in today's reading. It is a 'blessed hope', not a dreadful one. Christians have no fear in waiting since their salvation is secure. The hope we have is the hope that God's good purposes for us and His creation will at last be realised.

This 'blessed hope' consists of 'the glorious appearing' of Christ (v.13). Such terminology was usually used in Paul's world to describe the arrival of the Roman emperor. Today it's not so much royalty as celebrities who make glorious appearances. But the most glorious entrance any celebrity has ever made will be totally eclipsed by the coming of Christ. True splendour and majesty belong to Him alone (see 1 Tim. 6:14–16).

The second thing that makes the difference to waiting is *how we do it*. We can wait passively, whiling away the time; distractedly, filling the space with empty activity; impatiently, trying to hurry up what won't be hurried; or actively and patiently. Paul tells us active patience is the correct stance to adopt. Some early Christians expected the second coming to occur immediately so they gave up working and relied on others for support (2 Thess. 3:11–12). But that's the wrong thing to do. Rather, we should be busily serving Christ and cultivating holiness. Paul says we should be saying, '"No" to ungodliness and worldly passions' and living 'self-controlled, upright and godly lives in this present age' (v.12). Similarly, he told the Thessalonians that they were to 'never tire of doing what is right' (2 Thess. 3:13). It's the same message as we heard from Peter and John. So we are not to disengage with normal life or step out of our needy world and enter into some type of prolonged spiritual retreat until Christ returns. Instead we should take our coats off, roll our sleeves up and get stuck in as active and growing disciples.

So let's learn the art of true waiting – waiting actively for the most glorious future event we can contemplate.

To consider or discuss

- How do I react when I have to wait? What can I learn from Titus about what I need to do to wait in the right way for the return of Christ?

For group discussion

Moving on from the preparation involved in Christ's first coming, this week's studies concerned the way in which we need to prepare for His second coming – a doctrine which, once popular, has almost been forgotten by the Church today. Share with each other what teaching you have heard and what attention you've given to the subject recently.

1 What place does the thought of the second coming of Christ occupy in your Christian life? Do you share the eager expectation of the early Christians at His return? If not, why not?
2 How would you answer the sceptics who say the second coming will never happen?
3 Read 1 Thessalonians 4:13–5:11, which is some of the earliest teaching about this theme. What does it add to the passages we've studied this week about Christ's return?
4 Paul says 'encourage each other with these words' (1 Thess. 4:18). Discouragements to the Christian life abound. What can you say to encourage each other to be faithful and hopeful disciples as you welcome in the new year?

To guide your praying

Here are some New Testament prayers for Christ's coming again to use as the basis for your own praying that His return may not be delayed.

'Your kingdom come' (Matt. 6:10).

Marana tha (Aramaic) – 'Come, O Lord' (1 Cor. 16:22).

'"Behold, I am coming soon! My reward is with me, and I will give to everyone according to what they have done. I am the Alpha and the Omega, the First and the Last, the Beginning and the End" ... The Spirit and the bride say, "Come!" ... He who testifies to these things says, "Yes, I am coming soon." Amen. Come, Lord Jesus' (Rev. 22:12,17,20).

National Distributors

UK: (and countries not listed below)
CWR, Waverley Abbey House, Waverley Lane, Farnham, Surrey GU9 8EP. Tel: (01252) 784700
Outside UK (44) 1252 784700 Email: mail@cwr.org.uk

AUSTRALIA: KI Entertainment, Unit 21 317-321 Woodpark Road, Smithfield, New South Wales 2164.
Tel: 1 800 850 777 Fax: 02 9604 3699 Email: sales@kientertainment.com.au

CANADA: David C Cook Distribution Canada, PO Box 98, 55 Woodslee Avenue, Paris, Ontario
N3L 3E5. Tel: 1800 263 2664 Email: sandi.swanson@davidccook.ca

GHANA: Challenge Enterprises of Ghana, PO Box 5723, Accra. Tel: (021) 222437/223249
Fax: (021) 226227 Email: ceg@africaonline.com.gh

HONG KONG: Cross Communications Ltd, 1/F, 562A Nathan Road, Kowloon. Tel: 2780 1188
Fax: 2770 6229 Email: cross@crosshk.com

INDIA: Crystal Communications, 10-3-18/4/1, East Marredpalli, Secunderabad – 500026, Andhra
Pradesh. Tel/Fax: (040) 27737145 Email: crystal_edwj@rediffmail.com

KENYA: Keswick Books and Gifts Ltd, PO Box 10242-00400, Nairobi. Tel: (254) 20 312639/3870125
Email: keswick@swiftkenya.com

MALAYSIA: Canaanland, No. 25 Jalan PJU 1A/41B, NZX Commercial Centre, Ara Jaya, 47301 Petaling
Jaya, Selangor. Tel: (03) 7885 0540/1/2 Fax: (03) 7885 0545 Email: info@canaanland.com.my

Salvation Book Centre (M) Sdn Bhd, 23 Jalan SS 2/64, 47300 Petaling Jaya, Selangor.
Tel: (03) 78766411/78766797 Fax: (03) 78757066/78756360 Email: info@salvationbookcentre.com

NEW ZEALAND: KI Entertainment, Unit 21 317-321 Woodpark Road, Smithfield, New South Wales
2164, Australia. Tel: 0 800 850 777 Fax: +612 9604 3699 Email: sales@kientertainment.com.au

NIGERIA: FBFM, Helen Baugh House, 96 St Finbarr's College Road, Akoka, Lagos.
Tel: (01) 7747429/4700218/825775/827264 Email: fbfm_1@yahoo.com

PHILIPPINES: OMF Literature Inc, 776 Boni Avenue, Mandaluyong City. Tel: (02) 531 2183
Fax: (02) 531 1960 Email: gloadlaon@omflit.com

SINGAPORE: Alby Commercial Enterprises Pte Ltd, 95 Kallang Avenue #04–00, AIS Industrial Building,
339420. Tel: (65) 629 27238 Fax: (65) 629 27235 Email: marketing@alby.com.sg

SOUTH AFRICA: Struik Christian Books, 80 MacKenzie Street, PO Box 1144, Cape Town 8000.
Tel: (021) 462 4360 Fax: (021) 461 3612 Email: info@struikchristianmedia.co.za

SRI LANKA: Christombu Publications (Pvt) Ltd, Bartleet House, 65 Braybrooke Place, Colombo 2.
Tel: (9411) 2421073/2447665 Email: dhanad@bartleet.com

USA: David C Cook Distribution Canada, PO Box 98, 55 Woodslee Avenue, Paris, Ontario N3L 3E5,
Canada. Tel: 1800 263 2664 Email: sandi.swanson@davidccook.ca

Courses and seminars

Publishing and new media

Conference facilities

Transforming lives

CWR's vision is to enable people to experience personal transformation through applying God's Word to their lives and relationships.

Our Bible-based training and resources help people around the world to:
• Grow in their walk with God
• Understand and apply Scripture to their lives
• Resource themselves and their church
• Develop pastoral care and counselling skills
• Train for leadership
• Strengthen relationships, marriage and family life and much more.

Our insightful writers provide daily Bible-reading notes and other resources for all ages, and our experienced course designers and presenters have gained an international reputation for excellence and effectiveness.

CWR's Training and Conference Centre in Surrey, England, provides excellent facilities in an idyllic setting – ideal for both learning and spiritual refreshment.

 CWR Applying God's Word
to everyday life and relationships

CWR, Waverley Abbey House,
Waverley Lane, Farnham,
Surrey GU9 8EP, UK

Telephone: **+44 (0)1252 784700**
Email: **info@cwr.org.uk**
Website: **www.cwr.org.uk**

Registered Charity No 294387
Company Registration No 1990308

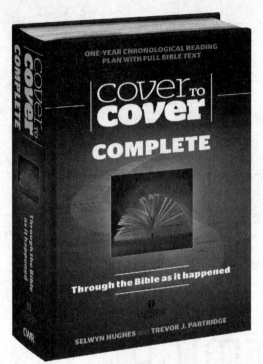

Journey through the Bible as it happened in a year of daily readings

Read through the entire Bible in a year with 366 daily readings from the Holman Christian Standard version, arranged in chronological order.

Beautiful charts, maps, illustrations and diagrams make the biblical background vivid, timelines enable you to track your progress, and daily commentary helps you to apply what you read to your life.

And a special website provides character studies, insightful articles, photos of archaeological sites and much more for increased understanding and insight.

Cover to Cover Complete
1,600-page hardback with ribbon marker, 140x215mm
ISBN: 978-1-85345-433-2